JOURNEY

RAINFOREST

MIND

A FIELD GUIDE FOR

GIFTED ADULTS AND TEENS, BOOK LOVERS,
OVERTHINKERS, GEEKS, SENSITIVES, BRAINIACS,
INTUITIVES, PROCRASTINATORS,
AND PERFECTIONISTS

PAULA PROBER

Licensed Psychotherapist

LUMINARE PRESS

WWW.LUMINAREPRESS.COM

JOURNEY INTO YOUR RAINFOREST MIND: A FIELD GUIDE FOR GIFTED ADULTS AND TEENS, BOOK LOVERS, OVERTHINKERS, GEEKS, SENSITIVES, BRAINIACS, INTUITIVES, PROCRASTINATORS, AND PERFECTIONISTS
© 2019 by Paula Prober

Printed in the United States of America

Cover Design: Claire Flint Last
Editing: Lori Stephens

Luminare Press
442 Charnelton St., Eugene, OR 97401
www.luminarepress.com

LCCN: 2019905216
ISBN: 978-1-64388-104-1

For the sensitive, creative,
persnickety, gifted souls with whom
I've had the honor to meet in my counseling
and consulting practice and on my blog.

Thank you for your courage, trust,
humor, and compassion. Keep seeking
your authenticity and spreading your love.
It can change everything.

CONTENTS

PREFACE VII

INTRODUCTION 1

1. What Is a Rainforest Mind? 8

2. What Are the Issues? 15

3. I'm Not Gifted, I'm Just Lucky 26

4. Too Sensitive, Too Dramatic,
   Too Intense 36

5. So Many Worries, So Little Time 46

6. Underwhelmed and Overwhelmed 53

7. Afflicted with Too Much Talent 63

8. Pressure, Potential, Procrastination, and Perfectionism 74

9. If I'm So Smart, Why Am I So Lonely? 90

10. Mortified by Mediocrity 99

11. Social Responsibility and Your Bad Hair Days 108

12. My Smart Kid Is So Emotional—Am I a Parenting Failure? 120

13. If I'm So Smart, Why Do I Need Psychotherapy? 135

14. The Good News 146

EPILOGUE 154

FURTHER READING AND RESOURCES 157

INDEX 161

Preface

I have been blogging for five years and have received many requests from readers to organize my most popular posts into a book. Readers were also interested in doing more inner work to better understand themselves. This book is that guide. It is also a companion to my first book, *Your Rainforest Mind: A Guide to the Well-Being of Gifted Adults and Youth*. While my first book was a deep dive into the rainforest mind, including many case studies of clients in therapy, this book is a more light-hearted look at giftedness in adults and youth. It is a faster read and a book that can be more easily handed off to relatives, friends, educators, medical professionals, and therapists or anyone who needs more understanding of the intense, sensitive, complex, curious, rainforest-y soul that is you.

As you might imagine, it is an act of faith (hubris? insanity?) for me to write a second book for highly intelligent, deep-thinking and feeling persnickety perfectionists. Apologies in advance, then, for grammatical errors, typos, inadequately researched assumptions, simplifications, inconsistencies, repetitions, and omissions. Thank you for your patience, tolerance, and grace.

Paula Prober

Introduction

Have you been told that you are too sensitive, too dramatic, too verbal, too smart, too curious, and too intense? Have you been called a know-it-all, geek, nerd, show-off, bookworm, crybaby, drama queen, or brainiac?

Have you been told that you are lucky you are so smart, you can do anything, and you have such great potential, but you are so overwhelmed by options, you don't choose anything?

❑ Do you feel pressure to be a high achiever but find yourself procrastinating and paralyzed by an extreme fear of failure?

❑ Do you love learning, research, and reading but have trouble navigating within the school system?

❑ Do you feel like you're *not enough* and *too much* at the same time?

❑ Do you ask yourself, *If I'm so smart, why am I so dumb?*

Yes? Chances are you have a "rainforest mind"—a mind that runs faster, wider, and deeper than most, a personhood that is highly sensitive, perceptive, and empathetic. Like the tropical rainforest, you are intense, extremely complex, full of life, and misunderstood. Like the rainforest, you have the ability to make a significant contribution to society, but you are being cut down before you can find your way.

The rainforest mind analogy is a way to describe a type of giftedness. If people are compared to ecosystems, then people as meadows, deserts, and oceans are all valuable and beautiful. One is not better than another. It is just that the rainforest ecosystem is the most complex, and it is being destroyed every day. We might compare this to our gifted individuals who are suffering when we misunderstand and misdiagnose them.

There is a lot of disagreement around what giftedness is. Is it talent? High achievement? Motivation? Eminence? Wiring? Genetics? Effort? Grit? Ten thousand hours of practice? In this book, I am not making a case for a one-and-only definition. I am writing about and for a particular type of gifted human: the rainforest-minded type who is sensitive, empathetic, intuitive, creative, analytical, multitalented, curious, highly intelligent, perceptive, and socially conscious. Other gifted individuals might be more cognitive and less empathetic, more linear/sequential and less creative. More singular focused. Talented in one particular field. For the purposes of this book, they will not be the focus, although there are clearly overlapping issues.

WHY THIS BOOK?

In my experience with gifted children and adults over the past thirty-five years as a teacher, psychotherapist, consultant, and blogger, I have seen how the gifted are misunderstood by educators, counselors, medical professionals, parents, and themselves. It is assumed that if a person is smart, they will be fine. They can solve their own problems. They will be successful, high-achieving adults. That is not necessarily the case.

There are intellectual, academic, social, emotional, and spiritual needs that these folks have due to their gifted traits, but there still aren't many resources or practitioners who understand them. More materials exist for gifted children, but there is still a lot of controversy. There are even fewer resources for these adults and teens.

This book is one of those resources. It provides information and explanations for rainforest-minded individuals and the people who work with them and love them. It provides tools, techniques, and exercises for gifted adults and teens. Professionals can use this book to educate themselves so that they are better able to serve this population.

Individuals with rainforest minds may deal with anxiety, depression, relationship issues, and career questions. Because they are deep thinkers and intense feelers, they bring a particularly complex dimension to their professional relationships. Often, they grew up with extra pressure to achieve, which can contribute to debilitating perfectionism. Many have had extraordinary frustrations with schooling because of their advanced learning abilities or have been bullied by peers and educators. Their extra sensitivities and empathy may leave them overwhelmed and in despair over the suffering of others. Their intense curiosity and multiple interests might lead to an inability to make decisions or select career paths. The need for intellectual stimulation often ends up as overwhelming loneliness. These are a few of the differences inherent in this population, yet the assumption is that they are "so smart" that they will be fine.

In my experience, they are often not fine. It is my hope that this book will be a useful, engaging, and enlightening resource.

MY BACKGROUND

I have been working with gifted children and adults for thirty-five-plus years, first as a teacher in public schools and teacher trainer/parent educator and now as a psychotherapist, consultant, author, and blogger.

I became an elementary teacher out of college and began teaching gifted children in pullout programs in grades 1–8. I was an adjunct instructor or guest presenter at local universities, training teachers how to work with gifted children in the regular classroom and parents how to raise these children at home. I began writing about giftedness for local and national publications.

I developed the analogy of the rainforest mind during those years to help teachers and parents understand giftedness. It also served as a way to address the concerns people frequently express about elitism.

In the metaphor, we agree that all humans have gifts, but they don't all have the same level of complexity, the same advanced abilities in multiple areas. It is a tricky topic and uncomfortable for many. In my years in the schools, in my counseling practice, and on my blog, I have known many individuals who struggle because they experience life differently. They can be accused of being too sensitive, too smart, too intense, too verbal, too curious, or too much. And this is true. The nature of the rainforest mind might be described as "more-ness"—more capacity for learning, more questioning, more emotional depth, more empathy, and more ability to perceive what others miss—but the "too muchness" is meant to be a put-down. It shouldn't be.

When I turned thirty-nine, I left the field of education and went to graduate school for a degree in counseling. Because I had spent years teaching gifted children, it seemed natural to open a counseling practice for the gifted. I saw how they had mental health issues that deserved particular notice and careful guidance. I now counsel rainforest-minded adults who struggle with self-esteem, anxiety, depression, relationships, grief/loss, and other issues resulting from growing up gifted in a dysfunctional family. I also consult with gifted adults internationally and with the parents of gifted children. I present at conferences and webinars and write for online publications including *ThriveGlobal*,

Rebelle Society, *Highly Sensitive Refuge*, and *Introvert Dear.*

I started blogging in March 2014. GHF Press found my blog and asked me to write a book for them; *Your Rainforest Mind: A Guide to the Well-Being of Gifted Adults and Youth* was published in June 2016. That book highlights case studies of former clients and their progress in therapy, understanding themselves as gifted adults and teens while also healing from trauma in their families of origin. It also includes comprehensive lists of relevant resources and strategies along with descriptions of the difficulties they face both personally and professionally.

Journey into Your Rainforest Mind was born out of the need for even more information on gifted adults and teens along with requests I received to organize the first four years of my most popular blog posts into a book. This second book will be useful as a faster, perhaps more entertaining read for the rainforest-minded but also for the people who love them and work with them.

The understanding of giftedness and the challenges that accompany these individuals' lives is still largely hidden. It is my hope that this book will contribute to the education of the gifted along with their relatives, friends, and practitioners so that gifted children and adults will understand and accept themselves, get their needs met more completely, and live lives of meaning, purpose, peace, and delight.

THE FORMAT OF THIS BOOK

This book is divided into chapters based on the most popular and relevant posts on my blog. Over the years, I have written about the topics that have been issues for my students, clients, and readers. These include misunderstanding what giftedness is, sensitivities, perfectionism, pressure/expectations, relationships/loneliness, impostor syndrome, anxiety, existential depression, social responsibility, dysfunctional families, and psychotherapy.

Instead of dividing the chapters by singular issues, I take a more holistic approach. The issues interrelate and overlap. Each chapter has a short introduction, two or more blog posts, and a number of exercises. For most of the workbook-type activities, a journal will be useful, as it could be beneficial to keep all your writing in one place.

I use the terms *rainforest mind* and *gifted* interchangeably. Not all gifted adults have rainforest minds, but all humans with rainforest minds are gifted.

CHAPTER 1

What Is a Rainforest Mind?

A s stated in the introduction, I created the analogy of the rainforest mind when I was teaching in public schools. I needed to find a way to explain giftedness to teachers and parents as I experienced it in my students. There was a lot of controversy around how to identify and serve gifted children, including whether to identify them at all. Gifted programs were seen as elitist and unnecessary. This is often still the case. Using the metaphor, we can honor all types of children and appreciate their differences. We can explain why children have a variety of educational needs without making one child better than another or more deserving. When I became a therapist and began working with adults, I expanded the metaphor to include gifted grownups, as the challenges the children face follow them into adulthood.

WELCOME TO YOUR RAINFOREST MIND

Like the rainforest, are you intense, multilayered, colorful, creative, highly sensitive, overwhelming, complex, idealistic and influential? Like the rainforest, are you misunderstood, misdiagnosed, and mysterious? Like the rainforest, have you met too many chain saws? If you answered yes to these questions, you may have a rainforest mind. Perhaps you're more familiar with the terms nerd, geek, bookworm, dork, or brainiac. Some of you may have been called precocious or gifted.

I use the rainforest metaphor because it cuts through the controversy. If people are like ecosystems, some are meadows, some are deserts, and some are rainforests. Each ecosystem is beautiful and valuable. The rainforest is just the most complex and maybe the most misunderstood—like you.

THE QUIZ

These are questions from my first book, *Your Rainforest Mind: A Guide to the Well-Being of Gifted Adults and Youth*, to consider as you decide if you have a rainforest mind.

- ☐ Do people tell you to lighten up when you are trying to enlighten them?

- ☐ Are you overwhelmed by breathtaking sunsets, itchy clothes, strong perfumes, clashing colors, bad architecture, buzzing that no one else hears, angry strangers, needy friends, or global hunger?

- ☐ Do you see ecru, beige, and sand where others see only white?

❑ Do you spend hours looking for the exact
word, precise flavor, smoothest texture, right
note, perfect gift, finest color, most meaningful
discussion, fairest solution, or deepest
connection?

❑ Have you ever called yourself ADHD because
you are easily distracted by new ideas or intricate
cobwebs, OCD because you alphabetize your
home library or color-code your sweaters, or
bipolar because you go from ecstasy to despair in
ten minutes?

❑ Are you passionate about learning, reading, and
research yet perplexed, perturbed, and perspiring
about schooling?

❑ Do your intuition and empathy tell you what
family members, neighbors, and stray dogs think,
feel, or need before they know what they think,
feel, or need?

❑ Do you find decision-making about your future
career and deciding what color to paint the
bedroom equally daunting due to the deluge of
possibilities assaulting your frontal lobe?

❑ Are your favorite spiritual conversations the
ones you have with trees, rocks, and babbling
brooks?

❑ Does your worth depend on your achievements so

that if you make a mistake or do not perform up to your standards, you feel like an utter failure as a human being now and forever?

❑ Do you crave intellectual stimulation, and are you desperate to find one person who is fascinated by fractals or thrilled by theology?

❑ Are you embarrassed to tell your family and friends that you find it easier to fall in love with ideas than with people?

❑ Have you ruminated about the purpose of life and your contribution to the betterment of humanity since you were young?

❑ Do you get blank, confused stares from people when you think you have said something really funny?

❑ Are people awestruck at what you can accomplish in a day, but you think that if they knew the real you, they would see that you are a lazy, procrastinating, slacking impostor?

❑ Are you afraid of failure/success, losing/ winning, criticism/praise, mediocrity/excellence, stagnation/change, not fitting in/fitting in, low expectations/high expectations, boredom/ intellectual challenge, and not being normal/ being normal?

❑ Do you long to drive a Ferrari at top speed on the open road but find yourself always stuck on the freeway in LA during rush hour?

❑ Do you love skipping down new sensual paths and exploring imaginary worlds to discover beautiful connections between fascinating objects, words, ideas, or images?

❑ Do you wonder how you can feel like "not enough" and "too much" at the same time?

❑ Are you uncomfortable with the label "gifted" and sure that if you were to use it to describe people with some sort of advanced intelligence—which you would not because it is so offensive—it would not apply to you?

If you answered yes to at least twelve of the above questions, you likely have a rainforest mind. If you ruminated about the answers to many of these questions and often thought "it depends," you, too, fit the profile.

WHAT YOU CAN DO

1. What do you think of the metaphor of the rainforest mind? Does it fit for you? If so, in what ways? Is there another analogy that better describes who you are? Write and/or draw your reactions.

2. How many of the quiz questions describe you? For each question that moved or surprised you, write examples of your experiences (or explain them to your partner or therapist). For example, do you feel frustrated by the slowness of others? Are you ever able to move intellectually at your optimum speed? What is it like for you when your coworkers don't appreciate your insights? What are some decisions that you are grappling with now, and how are you stuck because you're considering all the implications—and the connections between all the implications—and feel overwhelmed and cannot choose?

3. Can you imagine sharing the rainforest metaphor with others to explain your struggles? Who do you know who needs help understanding you? Imagine a scene where you share the quiz to start the conversation. How does it feel? What emotions come up? (If you are in therapy, mark the pages in this book that

you want to share with your therapist. If you're a therapist, you can use the quiz questions as a starting point to identify your gifted clients and have them share their thoughts, feelings, and experiences.)

4. Have you ever been called gifted? Many people are uncomfortable with that label because it's hard to know exactly what it means, and the specifics are different for everyone. Write about what "gifted" means in your life.

CHAPTER 2

What Are the Issues?

A dults with rainforest minds don't often see themselves as gifted. In this compilation of statements made by adults I have known, you will read of the confusion, denial, and misinformation that I see time and again. Look for signs of depression, anxiety, perfectionism, pressures to achieve, fear of failure, schooling frustrations, bullying, relationship difficulties, isolation, career choices, misdiagnoses, sensitivities, and social responsibility.

A RAINFOREST-MINDED ADULT SPEAKS

First of all, just so you know, I'm not gifted. I don't even like the word. What does it mean? Is it fair to say that some people are gifted and some aren't? The truth is it never did me any good to be labeled gifted when I was a kid. Yeah, they tested me for the gifted program in school, but I just got bullied, and I spent a lot of time waiting. Waiting for other kids to catch up. Waiting for the teacher to teach something I didn't know. Waiting to find a friend who could keep up with me. Who could understand me. I'm still waiting for that friend.

But I'm not gifted. I didn't get great grades in school. I'm not a walking dictionary. I wasn't the valedictorian. I even started failing classes in high school. There wasn't enough time to think. Sure, I got good test scores, but the tests were easy. Don't gifted people get all As all the time? I didn't always get As.

Really. I'm not gifted. I haven't won the Nobel Prize. I haven't won any prize. Well, there was the spelling bee in third grade. Does that count? I'm just a regular person. True, they called me a geek, nerd, showoff, and know-it-all, but geez, I don't know it all. Far from it. I'd *love* to know it all, but that's impossible. I want to learn everything about everything. I've got all of this unbridled enthusiasm about learning stuff. People find it annoying, you know. Why can't I be satisfied with a good football game or with watching *The Bachelor* on TV?

I know I'm not gifted. I worry all the time. Am I saying the right thing? Doing the right thing? I can't sleep at night because there's so much rumination. So many thoughts in so many different directions. I can't turn off my brain. Surely, if I were smart, I'd be able to stop worrying and figure things out. I'd be able to meditate easily and find enlightenment for heaven's sake, but no. There's so much thinking. They called me an overthinker when I was five, and I'm still overthinking.

I'm not gifted. I can't make decisions. There are always so many variables and variables within variables. I can't decide what color to paint the living room. I've painted it twelve times in the past four years, and it still isn't right. I still don't know what I want to do when I grow up. I'm overwhelmed by the number of interests I have. I changed majors four times in college and took seven years to graduate. Don't gifted people know what they know and take clear, confident action? Aren't they all prodigies and have a clear direction from the time they're born? Well, that's not me.

Look. I'm just not gifted. I tend to go from job to job, still trying to find my path. I learn a job in two years or less, get bored, and want to try something new. I have a resume that's all over the place. Coworkers aren't fond of me either. I get frustrated at meetings while I'm waiting for them to figure out what I told them at the beginning of the meeting or two months ago. I'm not patient or a good team player. Other people are lazy or don't listen to me. I get irritated easily. Not very gifted, if you ask me.

Anyway, it's too much responsibility. I mean, if I were gifted, wouldn't I have to change the world? Like Elon Musk, I'd have to build electric cars, send rockets to the international space station, and run a solar electric company. All at the same time? I'm just a mom raising a kid who is still throwing tantrums, and she's eight years old. She's so sensitive and so emotional. See, I'm a failing parent at that.

Really. Truly. I'm not gifted. I have high standards and expectations and think everyone ought to live up to them. No biggie. It's important to keep raising that bar, don't you think? How else will civilization evolve? I probably shouldn't take an hour to write a three-sentence email. That might be a teensy weensy excessive, but still. Standards, morals, ethics, expectations. I can't lower my standards.

I can tell you for sure that I'm not gifted. Professionals have told me so, and they should know, right? I've been diagnosed OCD, ADHD, and bipolar disordered, but no one has diagnosed me gifted disordered. Wouldn't my doctor and my shrink tell me if I had it?

I may be crazy, but I'm not gifted. I go nuts when the lights are buzzing and no one else hears them. When the leaf blowers are blowing. When I smell someone who needs a root canal. When I know someone who is depressed and faking it. I talk to trees, and they talk back to me. Crazy, right? Trees, rivers, birds—they're the sane ones. They're gifted.

I know I may sound intense. People say I talk too fast, but I'm cranking back my intensity right now, and I'm not talking as quickly as I'm thinking. Even though I'm not gifted, I may fit some of the characteristics of the rainforest mind. I can relate to that analogy. My brain does feel like a jungle. I'm complicated. Sensitive. Colorful. Maybe creative. Overwhelming. Dense. Green. I've definitely run into chain saws in my life. People have clearly wanted me to be cut down and turned into something I'm not. That's sad but true. Not that I'm complaining. I'm grateful for this life and for what I've got.

It's that sometimes, those chain saws. Sometimes they're too much. If I were gifted, which I'm not, but if I were, I'd want to send the gift back to the manufacturer for a refund. Unwrap the gift and send it back. Yeah. But I'm not gifted.

A RAINFOREST-MINDED TEEN SPEAKS

Hey, I'm Justin. I'm in counseling because my parents are worried. I don't have any real friends, and I spend a lot of time in my room or on the computer. My grades are dropping. I'm failing in a couple classes. They're afraid I'm depressed, maybe even suicidal. My parents are right to be concerned. I don't know what's wrong, but I've been a mess ever since I can remember, and lately, I've been wondering, *What's the point?*

I remember being in kindergarten, and I tried to talk with the other kids about stuff I'd read like the demise of the dinosaurs or how volcanoes work, or I'd want to show them the intricacies of the LEGO contraptions I built. They'd look at me like I was from another planet and go play in the sandbox, and I'd wonder what was wrong with me. What am I missing? How could they not love dinosaurs? How could they not love reading?

My teacher kept teaching about colors and shapes and counting to ten, and I'm thinking, *What about multiplication? What's wrong with me?* I was supposed to sit still and fill in the blanks on the worksheets when what I wanted was to know the size of the universe.

It's been that way for years. Sitting in a classroom, eager to learn something, anything, and hearing the same song over and over. I'm so disappointed in people, in teachers. I stopped doing the homework in some of my classes, and that's why my grades are so bad. I don't see the point of repeating something I already know. People tell me to just do it, but it's torture, and then there are the papers to write. Either I do so much research that I can't possibly put it all in a five-page paper, so I never hand anything in, or I know what I write won't be good enough, so I don't even start. They say I'm lazy. Am I lazy?

There is one teacher though. Mr. Grey. He keeps me in high school. He loves his subject, English literature, and he loves my curiosity and questions. He started a philosophy club where we could talk about film, literature, politics, anything. I'm usually the only one who shows up, but he's always there, getting my mind working hard, and it gives me hope. Makes life worth living. Someone who loves thinking outside the box, someone who isn't intimidated or offended or annoyed by my insatiable appetite for learning. Someone who makes me stretch my brain. I'm really grateful for Mr. Grey.

I used to be very emotional. I cried a lot, and my parents called me dramatic. I was very sensitive to noise, textures, and smells. I didn't like birthday parties because they were so chaotic. I could tell my parents were extremely uncomfortable with this, and that as a boy, I was supposed to suck it up. I cared deeply about things and was sad when I saw other kids getting hurt. I'm not emotional or sensitive anymore. No one knows how I feel. Funny, sometimes now people want me to tell them what I'm feeling. Most of the time, I have no idea.

I worry a lot. I worry about climate change, world hunger, poverty, racism. What can I do that will make a difference? Why am I here? What's the meaning of life? My brain never stops. It's exhausting.

You know, I just want someone my age to care, to think with me, to ask questions. God, I feel like such a freak. Our symphonic band went on a field trip to San Francisco. I was so excited to see the city, the art museums, the culture. All the other kids wanted to do was go to the mall. The mall. Like they've never seen a frickin' mall. I couldn't stand it and desperately wanted to leave the group, but I didn't want to create a scene, so I kept my mouth shut. People think I'm moody and disagreeable, but I'm just incredibly tired of trying to fit in and feeling like a fool. I just want to be normal. I just want to have friends. I'm so lonely.

I guess I should confess that I feel enormous anxiety when someone asks me to do something I've never done before and don't know if I can do it well and fast and the best. Like sports. I avoid sports at all costs, and I quit piano because you have to practice to get good at it. I'm used to being the best and getting approval for it, and I'm afraid that I'm not as smart as everyone says, so I don't take any unnecessary risks.

I need to help people. I can't stand to see people suffer. At the same time, I'm not proud of my record. There've been too many times when I watched someone get harassed at school and haven't done anything. I'm torn. I want to be liked, to be part of a group, to not be the school geek, but I leave school hating myself when I'm a coward. Someone is hurt, and I could've helped. Keeps me awake nights. I can feel their suffering in my heart.

People try and help me, and I appreciate it, but it's mostly inadequate. They come up with quick fixes and easy answers. I try and tell them gently that it's not that simple. It's never that simple, but they don't get it. Sometimes the only thing I find soothing is my dog and a walk in the woods. I feel a deep kinship with nature and a sense of connection with trees and the wind. I still cry at a perfect sunset.

I can't wait to get to college. Maybe there'll be kids there I can relate to, who will accept me, or maybe there'll be a professor in the music department who can give me the feedback I'm looking for. I'm in these bands at school, and I get these awards, but they're meaningless. I don't deserve them. I make all these mistakes that no one seems to notice. I don't get it. They tell me I'm the best trumpet player they've heard in years, but I know how much better I could sound. What I play is crap. They don't hear it.

Then again, I'm scared to death of college. I'm not sure what I'd do if I were put in a class with really smart kids. What if the work is too hard? What if I don't have all the answers? What'll I do? Who am I then? How do I study for a test? I haven't had to crack a book yet.

What if I can't get the answers fast? What will I major in? I have so many interests. They say I can do anything I want like that's a great thing, but all I feel is pressure and anxiety. How do I choose one thing? What if I'm not so smart and I've been able to fake it all this time? Maybe I won't go to college.

They say that I'm gifted, but I don't know. It sure doesn't feel like a gift to me.

WHAT YOU CAN DO

1. Write about your response to these soliloquies. How do you feel after reading them? What emotions were stirred up? What similar thoughts have you had? What different thoughts? If you're not comfortable with the label gifted, are you okay calling yourself rainforest-minded?

2. Write your own soliloquy. What would you have said as a teen? Now?

3. Write a list of the issues revealed in each soliloquy. Which ones do you relate to?

4. Why do you think you resist the notion that you are gifted? Were you teased or bullied for being smart? Do you fear someone will feel bad if you reveal how smart you are? Are you concerned with justice and feel it's not fair to say that someone is smarter than someone else? Do you feel normal and assume everyone is like you? Do you know how much you don't know? Do you question what "smart" is? Have you not achieved "greatness"?

5. Write a list of the traits that make you rainforest-minded. Include ways that others have described you. Check the list periodically as you read the book, and add or delete items as you learn more.

Paula Prober

6. If you are in therapy, write your soliloquy, and read it to your therapist. If you are a therapist, think of clients you may have misunderstood. How does knowing the traits of the rainforest mind change your perspective? Did you realize that many gifted folks deny their abilities and pathologize them? Keep reading to discover how you can support these clients as you get better at identifying them.

CHAPTER 3

I'm Not Gifted, I'm Just Lucky

There is a lot of confusion about what giftedness is. Even among advocates working in the field of gifted education, there are different views and opinions. Many of the clients I have worked with over the years are extremely uncomfortable with the label and do not identify as gifted. When I describe the analogy, they are willing to accept that they fit within the world of the rainforest-minded.

The following blog posts will give you a clearer picture of the reasons for that denial. They will help you understand some of the early experiences that may have influenced these inaccurate self-perceptions.

I KNOW HOW MUCH I DON'T KNOW

- I'm not gifted, the teacher likes me.

- I'm not gifted, I'm a good test taker.

- I'm not gifted, I barely passed calculus.

- I'm not gifted, this is easy.

- I'm not gifted, I haven't done anything remarkable.

Sound familiar?

What if you *are* g-g-gifted? Why do you feel you aren't? Why do you feel like a fake? An impostor? Why do you feel like you're sneaking by and one day it will all come crashing down?

As usual, with you there are no simple answers, but take a look at the following list, and identify which of these situations are true.

❑ You were praised a lot by your parents for your early achievements, so you now feel enormous pressure to perform perfectly, because your worth depends on it.

❑ You were told that you were smart over and over. You came to believe that learning anything should always be easy.

❑ School work was not challenging. You could procrastinate until the last minute and still get an A. The grade didn't mean much, because you didn't put in any effort.

❑ You were praised by your parents and teachers for things you felt you didn't deserve. You saw your mistakes and had higher standards for yourself than they did.

❑ You think you should know how to do many things without working at them or having to practice.

❑ You were singled out in school for your good grades and then bullied by your peers. You intentionally started to get lower grades.

❑ Your sibling was the intelligent one. You were the other one.

❑ You grew up in a seriously dysfunctional family, so your perception about who you are is distorted.

❑ You were criticized excessively by your parents, and now, even when you succeed, you hear their voices in your head.

❑ When you know how much better your work could be, you aren't content with your achievements.

❑ You didn't get good grades in school. You were highly sensitive and creative. Your intelligence wasn't noticed.

❑ You dropped out of college.

❑ You believe strongly in equality, so you try not to appear smarter than anyone else.

❑ You internalized racism and sexism, so you doubt your abilities.

❑ You got mixed messages about achievement. If you're female, you're not supposed to excel too much. You're told it's unfeminine and unattractive.

❑ When you don't work hard or don't have to struggle to achieve your goal, you can't give yourself credit for it.

❑ If you acknowledge that you're smart, you have a responsibility to contribute to creating a better world, and that responsibility is terrifying.

I know this is a long, odd conglomeration of things, but do any of them fit you? Many of them? A combination of these experiences could lead you to conclude that your achievements are not due to your intelligence and most unequivocally not your g-g-giftedness.

Which you don't have. At all.

WHY YOU STILL DON'T BELIEVE THAT YOU'RE GIFTED

People tell you that you're super smart. They're baffled by how much you know and how you know it. You can ace a test without studying. You can talk with just about anyone about just about anything. You're always thinking, analyzing, imagining and empathizing, but you're sure you're not gifted. How is that possible?

Here are some ideas.

- You know how much you don't know.

- You think you're normal. Doesn't everyone obsess about *Dr. Who* and David Attenborough's *Planet Earth* documentaries?

- Too many people have told you "Don't get a swelled head, "Who do you think you are," "You think you're so smart," or "Nobody likes a know-it-all."

- You value justice and equality. If someone is gifted, someone else is not gifted. It can imply that you think you're better than someone else.

- Your Aunt Mindy was gifted, and she didn't turn out too well.

- You haven't sent rockets into space or designed something "insanely great."

- You're good at faking it. If people knew the real you, it would be obvious that you're average.

- You've been told over and over that you can't possibly know as much as you know. You're starting to believe it.

- In school, it was embarrassing and lonely to be the smart kid. You'd have to live up to it, and the pressure would be overwhelming, and everyone would be disappointed in you, and the pressure would be even more overwhelming—so overwhelming that you'd have to disappear into a witness protection program and acquire a new identity, and not even Sherlock could find you.

- You fear rejection from family and friends. You want to belong, to fit in, to be normal.

- You have so many interests in so many diverse areas that you flit from topic/job to topic/job instead of mastering one topic/job thoroughly and completely for your entire lifetime. In fact, mastering only one topic/job thoroughly and completely for your entire life is terrifying.

- If you were gifted, you wouldn't be so anxious, so depressed, so not rich, or so bad at chess.

Why does it matter? Why do you need to realize that you are in fact gifted?

I'm glad you asked. It's simple. If you accept and embrace your giftedness (your rainforest mind), you'll be better able to find your authentic voice and contribute in your sensitive, intense, and complicated way to making a better world. Your Aunt Mindy will thank you! So will your kids, friends, partner, pets, colleagues, neighbors, trees, rivers, and planet.

I'M NOT GIFTED, I'M JUST WEIRD

You'd think that gifted people would know how smart they are. You'd think that they would find life smooth and easy. You'd think they would feel superior and judgmental of nongifted humans.

Nope. No way. Not the ones I know, and I've known a lot of them. I'm *that* old. (My former middle school students are turning fifty. Yeah. Old. Okay, old-ish.)

Granted, I work with a particular variety of gifted souls. Not all gifted folks are the rainforest-minded (RFM) type. Some can be cognitively advanced but not highly sensitive or empathetic. Some can be academic and scholarly but not have multipotentiality. Maybe some of the non-RFM gifted know how smart they are, find life easy, and are judgmental. Maybe.

They weren't in my classroom when I was a teacher in the seventies and eighties. They haven't been in my counseling office for the past twenty-five years. The RFMs I've known will tell you, *I'm not gifted. I'm just weird,* and they struggle with sensitivities and injustice. Decisions. Choices. Achievement. School. Relationships. Communication. Emotions. Careers. Belonging. Parenting. Anxiety. Depression. Perfectionism. Guilt. Politics. Climate change deniers. Conspicuous consumption. Not having enough time to read all of the books ever written.

That's if they grew up in a healthy family. If you throw a dysfunctional family into the mix, it gets even more complicated.

If you have a rainforest mind or love, teach, or work with someone who does, it's time to get out of denial.

It matters. Why?

It matters because everyone will benefit if RFM humans understand why they struggle and what to do about it. It matters because RFMs are raising RFM kids. If the parents know who they are, they'll be better able to support their children. It matters because educators, psychotherapists, doctors, and other professionals will stop misdiagnosing their clients and be more effective practitioners.

It matters because we all need the intelligence, compassion, creativity, and sensitivity that RFM beings share with us like we all need tropical rainforests.

We won't survive without them.

We won't survive without you.

WHAT YOU CAN DO

1. Go through the lists in this chapter, and check the items that apply to you. Pick the ones that stir up the most emotion, and write. Take your time. There is a lot here, so you may need to come back to it again. Much of it will be explained in later chapters.

2. In what ways were you advanced cognitively? Were you an early avid reader? Were you asking multiple questions that stumped the adults? Were you bored in school? How did school affect your understanding of your intelligence? We often assume that the smarter kids are the ones who get the best grades and the highest test scores. This is not necessarily the case. Did you grow up in a culture or family that didn't allow you to express your differences or your particular strengths? Was it important to be humble? Did you think that because you were struggling in school you could not possibly be gifted? Did you learn that highly sensitive people couldn't be so smart?

3. If you are a therapist, you can share these lists with your clients. Each list may be overwhelming, so take a few items at a time. Let your clients explain what the issue means to them. It will be a

great way for you to gain insight into what might otherwise take a lot of time to uncover.

CHAPTER 4

Too Sensitive, Too Dramatic, Too Intense

C hances are you are highly sensitive. Your sensitivities might be emotional, physical, psychic, spiritual, or all of the above. You may have deep emotional responses to situations and people. You may have to carefully choose clothing based on textures or colors. Medications may need to be prescribed at lower doses. You may be able to sense what people are feeling, have premonitions that are validated later, or have spiritual experiences.

Your sensitivities may be criticized or pathologized by family members, teachers, and therapists. Not knowing that a finely tuned nervous system and a body-mind that perceives more on multiple levels is part of your rainforest mind might lead you to believe that something is seriously wrong with you. The truth is these sensitivities are part of your personhood. Just as your intellect is larger, wider, and deeper, you feel and perceive subtleties that others miss. This perceptive ability is what contributes to your multiple intensities.

WHEN YOU FEEL EMOTIONALLY UNINTELLIGENT

How do we define emotional intelligence when we're talking about your rainforest mind? Maybe you feel that you are the opposite of emotionally intelligent. Here are some possible reasons.

❑ You feel emotionally UNintelligent because when you were a youngster, everyone told you that you were too sensitive, too dramatic, and too emotional.

❑ You feel emotionally UNintelligent because when you were a little tyke, you had frequent, flamboyant meltdowns.

❑ You feel emotionally UNintelligent because you're easily upset by fragrances, chemicals, clashing colors, social media, depressed relatives, ignorant politicians, leaf blowers, and bad architecture.

❑ You feel emotionally UNintelligent because you cry when you watch corny TV commercials, when you watch your child sleeping, when trees are cut down, or when you read an angry Facebook post.

What if the above are not indications that you are a histrionic, hysterical, neurotic, emotional cripple but are signs of your emotional maturity, expansiveness, and intelligence?

Let me explain.

A sign of rainforest-mindedness is depth. Depth, complexity, intensity. That means that you have big emotions. When your neighbor feels sad, you feel despair. When your uncle feels happy, you feel joyful. When your partner feels angry, you feel rage. When your classmate feels bored, you feel desperation. When your friend feels nothing, you feel awestruck. See what I mean?

These feelings aren't purposeless. No siree. They make you perceptive, insightful, and compassionate.

That said, your emotions might overwhelm you. They may get out of control or stuck. You might feel like you're drowning, lost, paralyzed, sick, anxious, depressed, or frightened.

If that happens, there are things you can do.

The despair, the joy, the rage, the desperation, the awestruck-ness? None of these make you emotionally UNintelligent. They make you gifted.

SENSITIVITY AND COMPASSION FATIGUE

Compassion hurts. When you feel connected to everything, you also feel responsible for everything. And you cannot turn away. Your destiny is bound with the destinies of others. You must either learn to carry the Universe or be crushed by it. You must grow strong enough to love the world, yet empty enough to sit down at the same table with its worst horrors. To seek enlightenment is to seek annihilation, rebirth, and the taking up of burdens. You must become prepared to touch and be touched by every thing in heaven and hell.

—Andrew Boyd
Daily Afflictions: The Agony of Being Connected to Everything in the Universe

This would be you—am I right? Connected to everything in the universe, with your supersensitivity, empathy, and compassion, capacity to perceive more, question more, and feel more?

I'm guessing that you could do with less more-ness, less supersensitivity-empathy-compassion, but it's who you are. You're stuck with it. We need you. This planet needs its rainforest minds.

Are there any advantages to being able to "feel connected to everything?" How do you get through each day on the roller coaster of annihilation and rebirth?

You're not alone. You're a part of everyone and everything. Rethink your loneliness. Your connectedness allows you to know you're a part of the mysterious, magical whole. Tune into the magic.

Your connectedness is your superpower. Opening to it, softening around it, and welcoming it will bring more insight, intuition, and creativity into your life and the planet. Yes, there will be sorrow. Welcome it. Feeling the sorrow will also bring more insight, intuition, and creativity into your life and the planet. Believe it.

HOW TO GET THROUGH EACH DAY

Find ways to know and express your deepest self through an art form, physical outlet, nature experience, spiritual practice, nonprofit, or career path. Don't wait any longer. Turn your rage and despair into art. Dance it. Paint it. Write it. Sing it.

Limit your exposure to the news. Read novels instead of comments on Facebook.

Get support from others who have rainforest minds. Know your limits, and set boundaries when needed. Just because you're capable doesn't mean that you have to take care of everyone.

Nourish your sense of humor. Snarkiness, silliness, reading *Calvin and Hobbes,* and binge watching Steven Colbert can be beneficial.

These words from Lin-Manuel Miranda's speech at the Tony awards in 2016 will soothe your sweet, sensitive soul.

> *When senseless acts of tragedy remind us/That nothing here is promised, not one day./This show is proof that history remembers/We lived through times when hate and fear seemed stronger./We rise and fall and light from dying embers, remembrances that hope and love last longer/And love is love is love is love is love is love is love cannot be killed or swept aside./I sing Vanessa's symphony, Eliza tells her story/Now fill the world with music,*

love and pride.

OVEREXCITABILITIES: CAN'T LIVE WITH THEM, CAN'T LIVE WITHOUT THEM

Overexcitabilities: those pesky traits that make your friends roll their eyes, relatives recommend medication, and neighbors head home early. Maybe you talk fast and often about your passion for stackable brain specimen coasters. Maybe you cry over the Facebook video of the adorable four-year-old telling his mother why he must become a vegetarian. Maybe you imagine hundreds of ways your child could be abducted by aliens on a Sunday afternoon. Maybe you can't sleep because the room is too hot, the sheets are too rough, and the breeze is too loud.

Life in the rainforest mind is intense. You may feel like *too much* on so many levels. Too emotional. Too sensitive. Too analytical. Too verbal. Too enthusiastic. Too idealistic. Too curious. Too smart.

If you're male, this *too muchness* can be particularly humiliating if you're trying to "man up" or "not be a sissy" or impress your former-high-school-football-star-race-car-driving-ex-Marine boss.

What can you do? Are you supposed to shrink? Dumb down? Toughen up? Become a football-star-race-car-driving-Marine?

Hell no.

- Understand that you are not too much. You're gifted. Your emotions and sensitivities are as vast as your intellect. This can feel overwhelming to others and to yourself.

- Learn the difference between repressing your emotions and containing them. Decide where it is safe to be fully yourself and where it's not. Practice ways to gently contain your intensity through mindfulness meditation, deep breathing, exercise, visualizing an actual container, or writing.

- Find people with whom you can geek out: book groups, Meetup groups, university classes, conferences, fellow mountain bikers, chess players, hikers, art makers, etc.

- Practice self-soothing techniques to calm your nervous system and anxiety, especially if some of your intensity comes from painful childhood experiences. You may need these techniques if your empathy is running amok, which it probably is.

- Use your sensitivities in your job or at home to understand your colleagues/children, create a more compassionate climate, gain insight, and solve problems more holistically.

- Imagine how the world would be a better place if more people were deeply sensitive and empathetic. Be a role model for children. Your *too muchness* is a strength, not a weakness.

Instead of shrinking, get larger. You heard me. Go more deeply into your heart, and feel yourself expand. Get as large as the universe. Feel your connection to all things. Let that connection hold you and love you. Become the universe.

Then go out and buy those stackable brain specimen coasters.

WHAT YOU CAN DO

1. Make a list of self-soothing activities to keep handy. What helps calm you? A warm bath? Classical music? Walks in nature? Building something? Make a list. It doesn't have to look like anyone else's list. Keep it handy, and use it!

2. As you appreciate your sensitivities, you will be more comfortable showing them. That said, there will be times when you will want to protect yourself from what may feel like assault or being misunderstood. There are apps that can help you with relaxation and stress reduction such as Calm and Headspace. Insight Timer has a large selection of guided meditations.

3. I mentioned doing art to express intense feelings. You don't need to have any talent. Try not to judge your work. See if you can put your perfectionism aside. This is art therapy, not fine art or art to share with others. It is just for you. It is meant to be messy and unbeautiful.

4. Let yourself say no when you need to. Give yourself permission to leave an event early or sit in the back or on the edge so you can make an easy escape.

5. About getting larger: come up with an image of expansion and safety. How might you feel your larger or Higher Self? Can you expand energetically using meditation? Do you lean against a tree and become one with it? What image helps you be centered and accept your sensitivities and intensities? Once you have the image, visualize it every day. Feel into it deeply.

6. If you are in therapy, talk about how your family viewed your sensitivity. Were you understood or ridiculed? What was that like? Did you feel your parents' anxieties and feel responsible for helping or that the tension was your fault? Were you given more responsibility than was appropriate because you were so capable?

7. If you are a therapist, read about overexcitabilities (OE) through the writings and interpretations of Kazimierz Dabrowski. *Living with Intensity* by Daniels and Piechowski is a good place to start. If you're a client in therapy, share some of Dabrowski's theory with your therapist. Describing giftedness as a set of OEs is a useful way to provide structure to the topic.

CHAPTER 5

So Many Worries, So Little Time

I have known many rainforest-minded humans who are anxious. Being extra aware, sensitive, and creative can be fertile ground for extreme worry and self-doubt. When you perceive multiple subtleties and complexities, there is more to be anxious about. When you see how everything is connected and you have a creative mind, it is easy to imagine disaster scenarios or catastrophize. Luckily, your imagination can also produce solutions, but a rich fantasy life can often lead to more monsters under the bed!

Because of your abundant sensitivities, it is likely that you have an easily activated nervous system. If you grew up in a seriously dysfunctional family, you may be hypervigilant as well. This would be the source of any extra anxiety. Add to that stressful events in the world, and your anxiety might be extreme.

THE MORE YOU KNOW, THE MORE YOU WORRY

Perhaps you thought that if you were smart, you wouldn't be a worrier. If you were smart, you'd know all the answers. You wouldn't have to be anxious because you could think your way out of any problem. You may worry constantly. You worry when you're sleeping. When you're hiking. When you're cooking. When you're driving. When you're not worrying. What's with that?

Let me explain.

Your active rainforest mind can dream up so many things to worry about. Less complex minds may worry less, because there isn't as much thinking. With you, there's lots of thinking, and if you're highly creative, watch out for even more worries.

Add to this your capacity to notice things that others don't. More to notice, more to worry about.

If you have deeply held ethical beliefs around justice issues and you're sensitive to the suffering of all beings, there might be a teensy weensy bit of anxiety in your world. See what I'm saying?

I understand that you think you ought to worry less, because as a smart person, you're supposed to be a great problem solver. Maybe you are a great problem solver. That may not stop the worry.

Of course, there might be complicating factors. Trauma in childhood might make you anxious today. Pressure and expectations due to your smartness might make you nervous. Hormone imbalances and illness might cause anxiety. You could be a parent.

Complicating factors. It's not easy to sort it all out, but I suggest that there's a connection between your rainforest mind and your capacity for worry. Because you think a lot, it's easy to slip into an anxious state. You have a mind that needs to be active, questioning, and dancing. Imagine that if you get more intellectual stimulation, you will worry less.

If all else fails, go for beauty. See the gorgeousness of the flower, the rainstorm, the laughing children, and the beauty of you—worries and all.

ANXIETY AND YOUR CREATIVE MIND

If you're a sensitive, empathetic human, which you know you are, it would be impossible not to feel somewhat anxious these days. Maybe very anxious. There are multiple reasons for this. I don't need to tell you there are many opportunities for anxiety.

You were born worrying. That busy mind of yours could think of endless possibilities for concern. The pterodactyl hiding under your bed. Those timed tests in school. Your friends' drug problems. The bullies on the street corner. The purpose of dark matter, not to mention your finely tuned, vividly accessible imagination. So many worries, so little time.

Then, if you became a parent, well, what were you thinking? Parenting? Not the best job for the rumination prone.

Here's the good news. Your rainforest mind is not just here for apprehension, anxiety, and angst. Nooooooo. You, dear friend, have an enormous capacity to be inspired, to feel awe, to know wonder. This may save you.

You know awe. The night sky. An ocean sunset. Swimming with dolphins. The birth of your child. Listening to Keala Settle sing *This Is Me.*

Wonder can take you out of your angst even if for a moment. It can allow you to feel your deep knowing, that there's something larger, more beautiful, and more powerful out there and in you. Maybe you call it beauty. Maybe you call it love. Maybe you call it intuition. Maybe you call it string theory. Maybe you call it God. Whatever you call it, get yourself some awe. Let wonder back into your life.

It will soothe your worried soul.

IF I'M SO SMART, WHY AM I SO ANXIOUS?

Feeling more, sensing more, thinking more, knowing more.

Extremely sensitive to sounds, smells, tastes, colors, touch, emotions, weather, food, chemicals, energy, bad news, criticism, the invisible world, and beauty.

A mind that moves at warp speed, seeks meaning, analyzes the hell out of everything, wonders, generates gazillions of ideas, and watches itself watching itself.

A heart that weeps at the cruelty humans inflict on one another and on the planet.

A soul that yearns for knowledge, understanding, and love.

You wonder why you're anxious?

Okay then. Let's get practical. Your anxiety may

manifest in many ways. You want to strangle your neighbor who uses her leaf blower to clear her driveway every morning. The chaos at birthday parties leaves you and your child shrieking. Your active, creative mind imagining unending catastrophes. You can't stop ruminating about the sad story you heard on NPR. You have migraines, allergies, or insomnia.

What can you do?

Becoming ungifted is not an option.

WHAT YOU CAN DO

1. At public events, leave early. Move chairs so you aren't too close to someone. Breathe deeply, and imagine peoples' undesirable energy moving through you and out your feet into the ground. Let the earth transform it.

2. Move your body. When worried, we tend to freeze, and that only increases anxiety. Try moving. Walk, dance, shake, exercise, sing. If it works for you, get regular, vigorous exercise. Try the "nutritious movement" ideas of Katy Bowman.

3. For lots of specific techniques, read *The Anxiety and Phobia Workbook* by Edmund Bourne. Check out healthjourneys.com or Heartmath.

4. Start that meditation practice you say you're going to start.

5. In your journal, dialogue with your anxiety. Visualize the anxiety as a person, and be curious. Ask why it continues to hang around. What is it trying to protect you from? What does it need to calm down? You may be surprised by the answers.

6. Be aware of food sensitivities, hormone imbalances, or sleep deprivation. Naturopathy,

acupuncture, massage, or energy work can be helpful.

7. If you're a parent, don't take your child's meltdowns personally. Take time away from the kids.

8. Find your sense of humor. If you're alone in your car, scream obscenities at passing drivers. Avoid eye contact.

9. If you're in therapy, you probably know that events can trigger PTSD symptoms, and you might unconsciously reexperience trauma. You may feel anxiety that makes no sense. This is a clue that therapy might be needed. Therapy can help you identify the triggers and learn ways to cope and heal.

CHAPTER 6

Underwhelmed and Overwhelmed

One of the challenges that come with rainforest-mindedness are the contradictions. You can feel smart and stupid at the same time. You can feel overwhelmed and underwhelmed. While your sensitivities may mean you are easily overwhelmed by sounds, smells, energies, and chemicals, your thinking ability may lead you to feel underwhelmed: bored, frustrated, or impatient with slower thinkers.

Speaking of slower thinkers, chances are that at some point in your life you have been called an overthinker. It is not meant as a compliment. You may even call yourself an overthinker, wishing you could slow down or quiet your mind enough so you could sleep or be entertained by some mindless television once in a while. Your extremely active mind, whether overwhelmed or underwhelmed, does not stop, and that can be exhausting and embarrassing.

A GUIDE FOR THE UNDERWHELMED
AND OVERWHELMED

You're capable. You're fast thinking. You draw accurate conclusions when everyone else is still lollygagging. You're at the finish line when others are leaving the starting gate.

Your coworkers would benefit from your insight if only they could realize that it's insight. They don't understand your leaps, and you're tired of filling in the blanks, so you sound unreasonable or outlandish.

You're thorough. You're deep-thinking. You analyze the complicated ramifications when everyone else is preoccupied with shopping. You're scuba diving when others are water skiing.

Your friends and family members would benefit from your perceptions and sensitivity if only they could realize that it's your rainforest mind and not an obsessive compulsive disorder. You've been labeled dramatic, depressed, and delusional, so *you're* the one in therapy.

Sound familiar? Am I in your head?

You feel like a weirdo, like a freak, like you don't belong. You're overwhelmed and underwhelmed. This is especially true if you were a little tyke in a dysfunctional family. At an early age, you had extra amounts of empathy and intelligence, and you probably felt the weight of responsibility in the family. You still do.

Here are some ideas that might help.

Remind yourself that just because you have lots of

skills and abilities and you can solve others' problems, it doesn't mean that you have to step in and rescue them or take that terrible job or say yes to every request.

Do you hear me? Read that paragraph again.

It's great that you're so capable, but it's important to have boundaries and limits and to take time to nourish yourself. If you take care of yourself, you'll be better able to help when the situation is appropriate. Practice this phrase when someone (including your child) asks for something: *Oh. Interesting. Let me think about it, and I'll get back to you.* Take a breath, and think about it.

Remember that it is normal for you to be both underwhelmed and overwhelmed because of your effervescent, multidimensional, perceptive rainforest mind. Managing your smartness isn't easy. All of those mosquitoes, monkeys, and tangled vines. It is a very busy place.

THE CONTRADICTIONS OF GIFTEDNESS

"Do I contradict myself? Very well, then I contradict myself. I am large. I contain multitudes."

—Walt Whitman

It appears that Walt Whitman knew something about rainforest minds.

You are large. You contain multitudes, but how do you live with your multitudinous-ness when other humans find you overwhelming? *You* find yourself overwhelming. How do you manage the contradictions of your youness? The anxieties that often come with the complexities? Your desire to create a better world?

You are large. You contain multitudes, but does anyone really *see* you?

Do you ache to be seen? To be known deeply? To connect with another human to feel that glorious sense of known-ity? I'm guessing that you do.

Here's the rub.

If your capacity for learning and being is vast, other humans may only be able to understand parts of you. Not that they aren't trying. They may be trying, but they don't have the capacity. They aren't as large. They have fewer multitudes.

For example, you may hunger to study contemporary art, postmodern philosophy, celestial navigation, leather craft, multiple languages, permaculture, world religions, Argentine tango, and rock climbing. Today. In your spare time. For fun.

Large.

You may have sensitivities and intuitions that take you to deeper dimensions. You may see and feel mysterious energies that open you to other realities. You may have an empathy that allows you to know and feel others' emotions and needs. You may connect with a spirituality that doesn't fit within the expected parameters.

Multitudes.

How does a person like you get seen? Met? Understood?

Thought number one. Find people who can grasp a few of your multitudes. Maybe you rock climb with Cynthia, read Dostoevsky with Joshua, discuss postmodern philosophy with Latisha, and tango with Alessandro. This is not ideal, because I know that you want that one person who can be your everything, but the more multitudes you have, the harder that will be.

Thought number two. Find someone or something larger than yourself. You heard me. This might be a human, but it might be nature, as in viewing the night sky, climbing Mt. Kilimanjaro, or swimming with dolphins. It might be spiritual guides who speak to you through your writing or your dreams or via the devas in your garden. It might be energies from an invisible reality or a parallel universe. It might be your own Higher Self. It might be God.

Stop fighting with your largess. Relax into your multiplicity. When you feel like shrinking, don't. Expand.

Be sure to contradict yourself. Daily.

Make Walt proud.

THE WORLD NEEDS MORE OVERTHINKERS

Thinking has gotten a bad rap. If you do a lot of it, which you know you do, you're called an overthinker, and that's something you're told you're supposed to avoid.

I know people who are underthinkers. I bet you do, too. Don't you wish those underthinkers would overthink once in a while? I know I do.

Granted, you can think so much that you get super anxious. You can think so much that you don't score well on multiple-choice tests, because you can explain why all the choices are correct. You can think so much that you never finish painting your bedroom. You can think so much that you don't have time to sleep. You can think so much that you forget to tie your shoes.

Too much thinking can become a problem. We know this, but honey, you're kinda stuck with it. It's how your brain works. Your big brain is active all the time, so for you, it's not overthinking. It's just thinking. Or being. It's curiosity. Analysis. Wondering. Creating. It's the quest for the Holy Grail.

It's you being you, and yet your colleagues, friends, relatives, partners, teachers, therapists, and maybe even your children would like you to STOP THINKING SO MUCH.

Yeah. I get it.

Maybe you also tell yourself to stop thinking so much.

I think you need to rethink thinking.

Find ways to take care of yourself when your thoughts turn into anxiety or paralysis or sleeplessness. Give yourself permission to self-soothe, whatever that looks like for you.

Don't stop "over" thinking, wondering, creating, and analyzing. Seeking the holy. Being you.

1. Write about times when you feel overwhelmed. What in particular feels like too much? Sounds of leaf blowers? People chewing? Perfume? People's unexpressed rage? Make a list, and consider how you might avoid these things or at least limit their impact.

2. Write about experiences of being underwhelmed. School? Certain people? When have you had high expectations of someone who disappointed you? It can be confusing when you realize that what comes easily to you may be difficult for others. Do you feel surprise? Guilt? Impatience? When you attend events, do you bring something to do in case of boredom?

3. If you're frustrated at your workplace and looking for support, get a copy of *Rebels at Work* and join their community. The authors, Carmen Medina and Lois Kelly, write and talk about ways creative, complex thinkers can work to change the system. You will see that you are not alone and not delusional.

4. If you are a parent, it is especially important that you know your limits and take time for self-care. On Facebook, parents offer great advice at

Parenting Gifted Children and Hoagies Gifted Discussion Group.

5. If you are introverted, Susan Cain's book, *Quiet*, and her community provide support and suggestions. The website Introvert, Dear is also helpful. If you are extroverted, you may be particularly distressed. Because you have greater needs for interaction with humans and because rainforest minds can be hard to find, you may feel extremely underwhelmed.

6. If you are in therapy, tell your therapist when you are frustrated with the process or when you are worrying that she or he might be overwhelmed by you. If you are used to learning quickly and easily, therapy may surprise you, because emotional healing takes time, particularly if there is lots of trauma in your past. It may also take time for you to trust your therapist, because you haven't felt seen or understood before. You may be skeptical that anyone can help since you are usually the smartest person in the room. Ask your therapist to read this book. Discuss the parts that you relate to. Give the process time.

7. If you are a therapist, take time to ask your clients about the counseling process. Listen to their concerns and insights carefully. They will likely be sensitive to your moods and energy. Be wary of pathologizing their intensity and

overthinking as OCD, ADHD, or bipolar disorder. James Webb's book *Misdiagnosis and Dual Diagnoses of Gifted Children and Adults* is a good resource. If you often feel overwhelmed, consider referring the client to a therapist who is more comfortable with this population. Remember to care for yourself.

CHAPTER 7

Afflicted with Too Much Talent

W hen you have many interests and abilities, also
called multipotentiality, decision making can
be tricky. You may feel like a jack-of-all-trades-
master-of-none or a dilettante. It can look like you are
doing many different jobs or projects or school majors
without depth and not finishing one before moving
on to the next. You might be seen as flakey, shallow,
or flighty.

Like life in the rainforest, it is not that simple. Many
humans are looking for their one great career or job they
can do for a lifetime. It is unusual to have many dispa-
rate career paths or great numbers of varied passions
and skills, but that is the nature of the rainforest mind.
It is not pathological or dysfunctional. You need help
understanding what it is and managing your multiplicity.

YOU'RE SO LUCKY, YOU CAN DO
ANYTHING YOU WANT

When you were a teen, did you hear this? *"You're so
lucky. You can do anything you want when you grow*

up. You could be a doctor, lawyer, musician, engineer, professor, IT professional, journalist, artist, or anthropologist—anything. Aren't you lucky!"

You didn't feel lucky. You felt confused and overwhelmed. Guilty and ungrateful. Paralyzed. A failure. Did I mention that you didn't feel lucky?

What happened to that kid who used to be full of excitement and enthusiasm? Reading voraciously. Sleeping with the encyclopedia. Dancing spontaneously. Curious beyond measure. What happened?

Let me guess.

Maybe it was school. Maybe it was your dysfunctional family and your chain saw parents. You're complicated, so it was probably more than one thing. For today, let's look at your unending number of interests and abilities. Your passion for learning new things. Your boredom with something once you've mastered it. Your multipotentiality.

You are afflicted with multipotentiality, or as Emilie Wapnick calls it in her TED talk, you're a multipotentialite.

Yes, indeed. I've known many rainforest-minded folks with this affliction, and you won't get any sympathy from the masses. Too much talent doesn't bring out the compassion, but for you, it can stop you in your tracks. How do you choose one thing? How do you make a career out of psychoneuromusicalanthrobiocomedy, not to mention being a psychoneuromusicalanthrobiocomedic parent?

Your coping strategies? Procrastination. Depression. Anxiety. Hot fudge sundaes. Not so great. To develop better coping strategies, know the following:

- You don't have to stick to one job/career. As a multipotentialite, it's appropriate to have a varied and rich resume.

- Multipotentiality is not a sign of weakness, inability to focus, ADHD, or slackeritis. It's a sign of rainforest-mindedness.

- You don't have to feel guilty anymore for your abundance. It's not your fault. You were born that way.

ARE YOU A MULTIPOTENTIALITE?

I am not a multipotentialite, but I've known many. I lived with one. Most of my counseling clients and several friends fit the bill. I suspect that I'm not one, so I can help you who are. If I were, things could get messy.

For those of you who are new to the term, let me explain. In an earlier post, I described how you may be overwhelmed by your extraordinary curiosity. You may, in fact, be as capable in the field of chemistry as you are in philosophy or as skilled in music as you are in literature, and you want to do it all. Depth and diversity are exciting, stimulating, and necessary.

You're afflicted with multipotentiality. Thus, you are a multipotentialite.

You may be like my client. I'll call her Rachel. She was interested in writing, sociology, literature, theology, politics, international relations, medicine, parenting, public speaking, feminism, and math. For starters. At age twenty-five, she was working in admissions at a university. It was a secure job with good benefits. She enjoyed it at first as she learned the ropes, did lots of public speaking, and traveled internationally. After about three years, there was nothing new to learn, and she grew frustrated. She came to counseling, looking for guidance.

It became apparent that Rachel was intellectually gifted (like many multipotentialites). She was highly sensitive, articulate, an avid reader, creative, perfectionistic, passionate about learning, analytical, fast thinking, and intense. When I explained multipotentiality, she was distressed and said, *"It's shattering to realize that there's not the shining beacon of a single path."* She felt lost in *"a shadowy, empty forest that had too many paths that went off far into the foggy distance."*

Knowing that she was a multipotentialite was not good news. She had to grieve the notion that she had one particular calling and that all she had to do was find it and do it. Multipotentiality was so much more complicated and frightening.

As we talked more, she began to accept and appreciate her gifted rainforest mind. We started planning her next career move. I suggested she read Barbara Sher's *Refuse to Choose*, examine other resources, and join Emilie Wapnick's community. She began to see that being a multipotentialite could work, but she was torn between being practical and going for her dreams. She was afraid that she was hoping for some unreachable "pie in the sky."

I asked her to consider that there was pie available, and she didn't have to go to the sky to get it.

SO MANY CAREER PATHS, SO LITTLE TIME

"If I had ten lives, I wouldn't be able to do everything I wanted to."

"My problem is I love to learn a job, then I optimize the job to do it in the fastest possible way, then I'm bored, and I want to move on to something else."

"Sometimes, there are so many things that I want to do, it's paralyzing, and I end up doing nothing."

Sound familiar? Could this be you? If it is, you may suffer from multipotentiality, a condition that afflicts many of the rainforest-minded. You may think that you skim the surface and never dive.

Maybe.

What if it's that you're fascinated by anthropology and gardening and researching and mathematics and art history and sustainability and—well, you get the idea.

How do you choose? What gets left behind? How do you explain to your parents that you're changing your college major for the fifth time? How do you explain to your friend Amy that you're bereft because you have to choose engineering over music? How do you explain to yourself why you're still working at Starbucks? How can such a smart person be so confused?

How many times have you heard *"Just pick something. Anything."*

Oh boy. You would if you could. It's hard for others to understand that you *love* learning new things, and you learn them quickly.

The possible career paths are overwhelming. Friends look at you quizzically. *"This is a problem?"* YES. It is, but how do you choose when you want to do it all? How do you choose when you'll lose interest in a year? How do you explain that you're not ungrateful but that you have to avoid boredom at all costs?

Remember this: You can walk many paths over your lifetime. You have a right to a work life that is meaningful, purposeful, and intellectually stimulating and, as David Whyte says, *"To wake the giant inside ourselves, we have to be faithful to our own eccentric nature, and bring it into conversation with the world."*

MISTAKES WILL MAKE YOU MORE LIKABLE

"If I'm so smart, why can't I make a decision?"

You would think that a smart person would find decision making easy, but, no, it's often quite the opposite. There are gazillions of reasons for this. Well, maybe not gazillions, but lots. Here are a few.

- You want to make the right decision, but you can think of arguments for all sides of the issue.

- You see how everything is related to everything else.

Paula Prober

- You're not sure which choice is the most in line with your ethical stance, and ethics matter.

- You want to choose the right thing, but then you have to let go of all the other things you didn't choose, and that's painful.

- You're concerned about how your decisions will affect others—not just family members but everyone.

- You're easily overwhelmed by the number of options.

- You feel pressure to do the right thing because that's what everyone expects, and you can't disappoint them.

- From the time you were a toddler, you were tuning into what others needed and trying to please them. You're still trying to please them. You have a pile of books by your bed, but you can't decide which one to read first because you want to know everything NOW.

- You grew up in a chain saw family, so it was life-threatening or humiliating to make a wrong choice.

- You care deeply about social justice, so you want to be fair to everyone.

- You are a multipotentialite.

- You like keeping things open ended, because there's always new information on the way.

- You believe that you're a complete failure if you make a wrong decision.

- You're terrified of screwing up your children.

What can you do? Develop and trust your intuition. Write dialogues with parts of yourself. Meditate. Do tai chi. Spend time in nature. Build a spiritual practice.

Those ideas work well for big decisions. What about the everyday choices?

This is tricky. I've made a list of mantras that you can say to yourself when you need them. Keep the list handy. It helps to breathe too. When faced with a "simple" choice or decision, say one or more of these to yourself.

- No one will die.

- Mistakes will make me more likable.

- I can change my mind at any time.

- Perfection is overrated.

- Maybe I was never prom queen/king, but I'm still an extremely cool person.

- My kids will grow up healthier if I model resilience.

- I can comfort the child part of me who is freaking out. The adult part of me knows what to do.

- It's all a grand experiment.

- I am a dynamic work of art in progress.

- No one else will even notice.

- I'm more critical of myself than anyone I know.

- My memoir will be much more fascinating if I make some ridiculous decisions.

If all else fails, remember the wisdom of Donald Antrim.

The simple question "What color do you want to paint that upstairs room?" might, if we follow things to their logical conclusions, be stated, "How do I live, knowing that I will one day die and leave you?

WHAT YOU CAN DO

1. Make a mindmap of your interests. They don't have to be practical or job related, just a map of activities and topics you love. Become more aware of how broad and varied your interests are. Write about how you've interpreted this and how others see you.

2. Look for the book *How to Be Everything* by Emilie Wapnick. She invented the term multipotentialite. She explains how you can craft a career plan that combines many of your interests. She provides examples and suggestions, and she understands your rainforest mind because she has one.

3. If you are a parent, make a list of all the ways parenting meets your needs for variety, emotional growth, problem solving, deep loving connection, and intellectual stimulation.

4. Make a list of all the things you have done so far in your jobs/careers and family life to prove to yourself that you have accomplished a lot (even if you feel like you have not).

5. Write about how it feels to have to leave some of your interests behind. Let yourself grieve over the choices that you do not take. Even though you can

do a lot, you probably won't get to everything in one lifetime. Write a eulogy to the career paths that have died. Believe in reincarnation.

6. Go to empoweryou.com, and read Laurence Boldt's *Zen and the Art of Making a Living.* Boldt says, *"Make your work an expression of love in action."* He provides resources for people wanting to have a positive impact on the world. He has powerful ideas and lots of fine philosophy.

7. For the poet in you, read David Whyte's books on work such as *Crossing the Unknown Sea: Work as a Pilgrimage of Identity.* His ideas aren't practical as much as they are brilliant.

8. Join Emilie Wapnick's group at puttylike.com.

9. If you are in therapy, you may have to explain multipotentiality to your therapist. Even career counselors and coaches may not have experience with it. Your therapist may be able to provide emotional support, but you may need to take the lead on this one.

10. If you are a therapist, read the books I have recommended, and educate yourself. If you have these traits, all the better. Your clients will be grateful when you don't pathologize them but support their desire for multiple career paths and experiences.

CHAPTER 8

Pressure, Potential, Procrastination, and Perfectionism

A nyone can be a perfectionist, but there are particular differences in the rainforest-minded varieties. The pressure to be smart and a high achiever can start early with well-meaning parents. Too much praise or overreactivity to accomplishments can send messages to children that they are loved for their achievements. If learning comes easily, children will believe that all learning must be fast and easy or something is wrong with them. The result is unhealthy perfectionism.

At the same time, there is a type of perfectionism that is innate and healthy. This comes from a deep, inborn yearning for beauty, balance, harmony, precision, and justice. It can result in the highest quality such as extraordinary art, exquisite technological innovations, elegant compassion, profound insight, powerful activism, or successful surgeries. If misunderstood, it can lead to deep frustration or self-deprecation. Both types of perfectionism require understanding and attention.

I HAVE TO KNOW IT BEFORE I LEARN IT

What if from the time you were two years old, you were told how smart you were? Over and over, enthusiastically, by (well-meaning) parents and doting relatives? What if they praised you repeatedly for your many achievements and your perfect grades? What if you could tell that your parents needed you to be smart, that they felt better about themselves because you were so capable? What if you were so persuasive that they gave you too much control and not enough limits?

What if when you arrived at elementary school, the work was too easy? You knew it before you were taught it. You learned things without trying. What if you could get perfect scores on tests without studying, and your scores were held up as an example for your fellow students? What if you were told by your teachers that you were the best student they'd ever had?

Do you think you might grow up terrified of failure? Afraid to disappoint others? Hiding mistakes? Paralyzed by anxiety? Believing that if you aren't a superachiever or the best at everything, you're a failure? Thinking that all learning must be quick and easy or else it means that you're not smart? You're an impostor? A fake?

Did you grow up thinking that you should know everything before you learned it so that practicing or studying or effort felt boring or scary or unfamiliar? That you had to be mature and adult-like at all times? That you couldn't tell anyone that you didn't know something because you had to know everything?

Well, my dears, this may be the root of your unhealthy perfectionism. This may be the root of your (possibly unconscious) belief that you have to be super smart at all times, or you're worthless and unlovable.

By the way, parents, relatives, and educators aren't conspiring against you. They don't realize the effects of their reactions. Responses like these are common.

Understanding this root is the first step in changing its effects.

So now what?

This is not easy to change, especially if you've been living with these beliefs for a long time.

Know this: You are more than your grades, your achievements, your intellectual abilities. So much more. You are worthy of love whether you write the perfect essay, win the competition, enter the elite school, get the high-paying job, make the right decision, or invent the iPhone or if you *don't* achieve these things.

Somewhere deep inside yourself, you know your worth. You know who you really are.

So here's an idea. Imagine that there's a place in you that isn't about achievement or accolades or winning or losing. This place is about love. Just Love. It's radiant and joyful. Maybe it's a young child part of you. Maybe it's an old wise part. Maybe it's in your heart. Maybe it's in your gut, but trust me, it's there, waiting for you to notice.

I'm betting that finding the love will soften you up. It'll remind you of what's really true and of who you really are.

DRIVEN PERFECTIONIST IN SLACKER WORLD

Angela is driven. At her job as a graphic designer and communications coordinator, she works ten-hour days and many weekends. Her standards for her work are well beyond those of her colleagues, including the CEO of the organization. Coworkers depend on her to keep the company functioning but also resent her high expectations, her critiques of their writing, and her evaluation of their less-than-adequate customer service.

Angela didn't attend college. She was raised in a seriously dysfunctional family. It's hard to understand how she knows what she knows unless you realize that she has a rainforest mind: a mind that learns quickly and deeply whatever it finds appealing, fascinating, or complicated. A heart that feels extreme empathy for humans, animals, and plants.

Coworkers take advantage of Angela. Because her work is always of the highest quality and completed in less than half the time, she's one person doing a three-person job. Not only that—workmates ask her to create invitations for their kids' birthday parties and design the programs for Aunt Matilda's half-sister's memorial. In her spare time. For free. She does it because she can and because she can't say no.

Angela is a driven perfectionist in a slacker world.

I tell her, *"Just because you're able to do it doesn't mean you have to do it. You have a right to set boundaries. To say no. To have a life outside of your job,"* but her extraordinary abilities, her empathy, and her early trauma all tell her no is not an option.

I tell her, *"Feel your satisfaction-sometimes-joy in finding the perfect phrase and the most striking images. Understand that others may not notice or care. Feel your satisfaction-sometimes-joy anyway."* This is the healthy perfectionism that comes with a rainforest mind. Regular people may not understand it.

I tell her, *"If you feel resentment, anger, or extra stressed at your job, consider allowing some of your work to be less than extraordinary. Settle for excellent. Notice if you need to excel because it gives you joy or because you have to prove your worth. Or both."* If it's unworthiness, it's unhealthy perfectionism. You can thank your dysfunctional family for that. Your therapist can help you detach your sense of worth from your achievements.

Well then. If you are like Angela, a driven perfectionist in a slacker world, take heart. Find the places where your drive, idealism, and high standards are appreciated and needed. Your favorite struggling nonprofit? Your gifted kids? Your community garden? Your elderly neighbors? Spend time in those places.

And your coworker's Aunt Matilda's half-sister? I'm pretty sure she won't mind if there aren't any programs at her memorial.

IF I'M SO SMART, WHY DO I FEEL
LIKE A FAILURE?

Was this you?

You were told repeatedly that you were smart, that you had a high IQ. You were the top student. Your parents and teachers praised you often for your abilities and achievements. School was easy, so you could get high grades without studying. You won awards. Teachers said that you were gifted. Your parents said that you'd do great things when you reached adulthood, that you could do anything you wanted. Expectations were high.

So was the pressure, but you didn't realize it until you got to college. Suddenly you were surrounded by smart kids. You were no longer the star. Not only that, some of your classes were hard; studying was required. Studying? What's that? You got your first C. You loved psychology and philosophy, but you'd never faced a workload like this. No one else seemed to be having trouble. You started procrastinating, as usual, but last-minute finishes didn't work anymore. It was confusing and overwhelming. Your identity was crumbling; you became anxious and depressed.

In your mind, it became clear that you'd been faking your smarts all these years. You weren't gifted. Never had been. You'd gotten by on your charm. Now charm wasn't enough. You were a failure. Every little mistake, every question you couldn't answer. Failure.

Is this you or someone you know? Let me give you a hug and an explanation.

Kids who are gifted are often told, repeatedly, how smart they are by well-meaning adults. High grades and other achievements are praised excessively. This can lead children to believe that they're loved because they're *so smart.* Their identity becomes dependent on their capacity to continue to show their advanced abilities and on the praise and attention they receive.

This can lead to unhealthy perfectionism: fear of failure, avoidance of activities that don't guarantee success, impostor syndrome, and procrastination. It can lead to anxiety and depression. Being smart becomes a static thing. You either are or you aren't. Because you are used to learning many things quickly, you think that is the way all learning should be. If you don't get it fast, well, it proves that you are not gifted. Not gifted? Not lovable. What can you do?

Understand that your worth as a human isn't due to your accomplishments. Your worth is about who you are, not what you do. It will take time to believe this.

Even if you feel discouraged and anxious some of the time, or a lot of the time, there is love in you. There is beauty in you. You can do this.

PERFECTIONISM'S TWIN SISTER

Continuing on our trek through the jungle—your wild, fertile, and colorful rainforest mind.

I want to get to the good kind of perfectionism. Yes, there is a healthy perfectionism. It can still drive you and your coworkers, friends, and relatives crazy. It can still stop you from starting a project or from finishing, but it's not something to discard, destroy, or disregard. It's an inherent part of your nature. You were born with this.

Simply stated: You strive for beauty, balance, harmony, justice, and precision in all things. (Well, maybe not *all* things. Maybe it doesn't apply to your garage.) Am I right?

I might add that this means you have extremely high standards and expectations for yourself. I say this with confidence because I have seen this *intrinsic* perfectionism in practically every rainforest-minded person I have ever known. I have been hanging out with them since the mid-seventies. That's a long time. That's a lot of people.

Are you often obsessed with an idea? Driven? Researching incessantly? Do you keep raising the bar when you reach a goal? When you were a child, did you fail to turn in assignments when they didn't meet your standards even when you knew you'd get an A?

See? What did I tell you?

What about this: When you see perfection in an ocean sunset or in a star-filled night sky, when you hear perfection in the music that you adore, when you taste perfection at that restaurant in Paris, does it take your breath away? When you find the exact word for the story, or when all the elements of your experiment line up just right, or when the poetry of the mathematical equation sings to you, is there a sense of satisfaction that is deep and unmistakable?

Yes? Good. Here's the problem: Other people don't get it.

It looks neurotic, dysfunctional, excessive, and OCD to them. Maybe to you, too. It's not, but it can get you kicked out of graduate school because you don't hand in your poems on time. It can mean that your colleagues don't invite you to join them at happy hour. It can mean that your taxes are four years overdue.

Did I mention that this might be a problem? How do you keep your vision, your idealism, your capacity for creating mental, emotional, spiritual, or actual cathedrals and still do your taxes, maintain friendships, or stay in school?

First, recognize that intrinsic perfectionism is part of who you are, and it means that with you, beauty happens. Quality is expected and produced, and this is a good thing.

Second, look for other rainforest-minded folks, and appreciate their high standards. Invite them out for happy hour. Get feedback on your work from people with similar expectations and abilities so that you respect and believe what they're telling you.

Finally, prioritize. Find the projects and activities that don't need to be exquisite or comprehensive or ridiculously awe-inspiring. Excellence can be enough.

Paula Prober

Good enough can be enough, on occasion, for the less important things. I mean it.

TAMING THE PROCRASTINATION BEAST

Smart people procrastinate.

Really? What do smart people have to procrastinate about? Can't they get things done with ease and aplomb?

Oh brother.

I realize that you may not be a procrastinator, and if you aren't, that doesn't mean that you aren't a smart person. I'm making a sweeping generalization, as is my tendency, because so many of the rainforest-minded folks I know are procrastinators. As I've told you before, I know a heck of a lot of smart people since I've been working with them in some form or another since the seventies, which I realize suggests that I must be close to geezerhood (which I am). Age aside, I still have a totally unscientific anecdotal experience of hordes of gifted people waiting until the very last minute to complete whatever it was that needed completing. Really.

For those of you who *are* procrastinators or have one or more in your home, I'm here to help.

First, let's get clear about the reasons why you procrastinate. In no particular order, do you ever think any of the following?

❑ **If I do it at the last minute and it's not great, it's because I didn't have the time.**

- ❏ I have to be brilliant all the time, or people will see I'm not so smart. They'll be disappointed in me, and I can't let that happen.

- ❏ My identity depends on my achievements. If I fail at something, it means I'm worthless.

- ❏ I believe that everything I do needs to be perfect.

- ❏ I could do assignments for school at the last minute and still get an A. Now I don't know how not to do things at the last minute.

- ❏ I never learned how to take one step at a time or prioritize, so I get overwhelmed by tasks.

- ❏ What I'm doing is so mundane, I can at least add time pressure to make it more stimulating.

- ❏ I can't be mediocre, ordinary, work hard, ask for help, or lose.

What do these thoughts have in common? Pressure. Expectations. Perfectionism. Performance anxiety. Patterns formed in childhood. A shadow side of being gifted. So what do you do?

First, you don't have to feel guilty if you haven't tamed your procrastination. In the best book I've seen on the topic, creatively titled *Procrastination,* by Jane Burka and Lenora Yuen, readers are told that the factors that contribute to procrastination are "not only individual psychological, behavioral, and emotional issues, but also social, cultural, and technological dynamics, biological, and neurological predispositions and universal human tendencies."

Oh boy. Now don't get all overwhelmed on me.

They provide several chapters of excellent suggestions, steps you can take to begin to tame the beast.

What else? What if you start to imagine that you do have a rainforest mind? You're highly sensitive, empathetic, socially conscious, emotional, creative, and intense. You analyze deeply. You think nonstop.

It's not good or bad. It just is. You just are. Remember this from the book *Procrastination*:

> *Confronting and changing long-held assumptions about you and your family can be unnerving and disorienting. This is why procrastination is so hard to overcome. It's not simply a matter of changing a habit; it requires changing your inner world. However, as you access capabilities and parts of yourself that have been held back by procrastination, you can derive great pleasure in claiming your whole self.*
>
> —Jane Burka and Lenora Yuen

WHAT YOU CAN DO

1. Think back to your early years. How were your achievements received? Do you remember feeling pressure to get good grades or accomplish a lot? Write about your experiences and your sense of how this pressure affects you now.

2. Write your response to this: *"Just because you're able to do it doesn't mean you have to do it. You have a right to set boundaries, to say no, to have a life outside of your job."*

3. Write your response to this: *"If you feel resentment, anger, or extra stressed at your job, consider allowing some of your work to be less than extraordinary. Settle for excellent. Notice if you need to excel because it gives you joy or because you have to prove your worth or both."*

4. Make a list of your values. What do you appreciate about others? Compassion? Generosity? Sense of humor? Can you admire these values in yourself?

5. Imagine your life as a work in progress or a form of artistic expression. Focus on the journey or the process instead of the product or outcome. If you are in school, design a plan for studying and completing assignments. Break projects

down into smaller steps. Look for resources online about dealing with procrastination, perfectionism, expectations, and fear of failure.

6. Learn about Carol Dweck's work on mindsets. Even if giftedness is the way your brain is wired, that does not mean it is an all-or-nothing phenomenon. You can still have strengths and weaknesses. You can make mistakes and still be a lovely human. You can have high standards and not be perfect.

7. Make a list of your thoughts and beliefs about your "failures." Are they rational? Replace your irrational beliefs with what's actually true. This is a cognitive behavioral therapy (CBT) technique. You can find out more about this in Bourne's *The Anxiety and Phobia Workbook*.

8. Read biographies of eminent people, and make note of their struggles, mistakes, and failures. Elon Musk and Steve Jobs failed multiple times.

9. If you are a parent, avoid praise. It is often meaningless. Instead, encourage your children by giving specific feedback and asking questions. *"I noticed how kind you were to that boy." "I'm enjoying the details about the characters in your story." "How was it for you when your team worked so well together?"* Encourage your child to engage in activities where they need to struggle.

They will learn how to deal with mistakes, failures, and setbacks and will form a stronger sense of self.

10. Imagine there is a place in you that is not about achievement, accolades, winning, or losing. This place is just about love. It is radiant and joyful. Maybe it is a young child part of you. Maybe it is an old wise part. Maybe it is in your heart. Maybe it is in your gut. Trust me, it is there waiting for you to notice. In a journal or in your mind, write to or picture this part of yourself. Take your time. You may be skeptical. You may need to meditate first or sit by your favorite tree. Write a letter to this radiance. Ask it to show itself to you. Ask it for help. Write or hear its response. It might come quickly, or you might need to wait for a while. Start a relationship.

11. If you notice that you have unhealthy perfectionism from growing up in a dysfunctional family, work with your therapist to understand it. It will take time to unravel the deep effects. Be patient. This type of perfectionism is tricky.

12. If you are a therapist, recognize how early responses to achievement can plant the seeds for deep perfectionism that will take time to soften. Your awareness of this will be a huge gift to your clients because it is so misunderstood.

Paula Prober

Explaining to them how they have an innate form of perfectionism that is something to admire will have a significant impact.

CHAPTER 9

If I'm So Smart, Why Am I So Lonely?

t is often hard to find humans who are similarly smart and sensitive. The literature about giftedness says that 3–5 percent of the population has these traits. This means that you spend a lot of time alone or with people who do not get you. Many of my clients and readers talk about how hard it is to find others who understand and welcome their sensitivities and intensities and can follow their intellectual musings and deep dives.

THEY'LL SEE YOU SPARKLING

It didn't go well when you were a child. You assumed that the other five-year-olds loved reading the dictionary as much as you did. You assumed that all seven-year-olds preferred a vacation to NASA over a trip to Disneyworld.

You assumed that the other kids would want to play your intricate games and learn your secret codes rather than play yet another round of Candyland.

You didn't know that you had a rainforest mind. Maybe you still don't.

That's why I'm here.

Relationships can be tricky when you have a rainforest mind. Have you noticed? You think you're explaining your ideas thoroughly and clearly, but your listeners aren't listening. They're lost in your creative leaps and poetic language, or they don't care about the future of the electric car. They think your enthusiasm for mycelium is weird. That *you* are weird.

If you're particularly sensitive (which I know you are), you're feeling more emotion and more empathy than the people around you. They might start avoiding you because you seem to be less cool, less able to "go with the flow."

You might find it hard to pretend to like them or to accommodate their need for chitchat. You might feel crazy because what's obvious to you might not be apparent to them, but you want to belong. You want to fit in. Have friends, for heaven's sake. Maybe even find a partner. Right? Is that too much to ask?

I have good news and bad news.

Good news: There are rainforest-minded people out there. I meet them every day in my counseling office. (Aren't I the lucky one?) They are radiant beings. Shining lights of smartness, courage, and sweetness. (Just like you.) Navigating their intricate and luminous existences on this planet. Seeking authenticity, purpose, and love. Wanting to make a difference while they're here.

Bad news: You will have to look for them. Carefully. They're probably hiding, like you are.

I have some ideas. Mostly, you have to know who you are. Figure out who you are. Use psychotherapy, yoga, meditation, painting, dancing, science, astrology, acupuncture, reading, hiking, music, spirituality, dark chocolate, or some combination of these things. It'll require time and effort. There may be crying.

Then you have to love that gorgeous, rainforest-y mind (heart-body-soul-spirit) of yours.

You can do it.

Take a moment now and feel your glow. Maybe it's in your heart. Maybe in your belly or your feet. I know it's there. It's always been there. It may be crushed under the weight of a dysfunctional family, inadequate schooling, global suffering, or some combination of these things.

As you feel your own radiance, you'll be better able to spot your cohorts, your mates, and your clan, and you'll have the courage to approach them and create your community.

They'll find you, too.

You'll be hard to miss.

They'll see you sparkling.

LEARN THE ARGENTINE TANGO

Are you looking for a way to meet people who are smart, sensitive, creative, and curious? Are you wondering where computer geeks, philosophers, physicists, musicians, artists, avid readers, and psychotherapists gather? Would you like to engage in an activity that will improve your balance, flexibility, and brain? Are you needing a way to get embraced by friendly strangers whose sole purpose in that moment is to tune into your beating heart?

Yes? You need the Argentine tango.

When I started dancing the tango at age forty-seven, I quickly became enthralled by the beauty, the music, and the sensual-osity of it all. Because I'm always on the lookout for rainforest minds, I was pleasantly surprised to find so many in one place. I think that's because the Argentine tango is both intellectually and creatively challenging to learn and very satisfying once you reach a certain level of competence.

Tango requires all those things that you already have: intelligence, sensitivity, curiosity, intuition, and empathy. It gives you something that you may not have: safe, sweet moments of intimacy with other humans.

I am not making this up.

You may have trouble finding people who want to travel into the depths with you. You may have trouble finding people who can keep up with your rapid thoughts and complicated emotions. If you're an avid reader, researcher, and writer like Maria Popova, the creator of the fabulous weekly online digest Brain Pickings, most of your friends may be *"dead people."*

Popova describes herself as "an interestingness hunter-gatherer and curious mind at large." Her website is, as she says, "a subjective lens on what matters in the world and why." She synthesizes the works of all sorts of great thinkers, authors, and artists (many of them dead) and draws her own brilliant conclusions. I'm guessing that she's got a rainforest mind. She was interviewed by Krista Tippett for her program *On Being* and asked to speak for her generation. (She was thirty at the time of the interview.) She said that she couldn't do that because *"most of my friends are dead people."* She's not spending much time with her generation.

Perhaps you aren't either.

If you're looking for some humans who are smart, sensitive, creative, and curious, and if most of your friends are dead people and you want to find some living ones, well, now you know what to do.

FIND YOUR PIPS

It's hard to find other rainforest minds.

They're not usually hanging out at the mall. (Okay, maybe *you* hang out at the mall.) They don't wear identifying clothing. They don't carry slide rules. (Okay, maybe *you* wear your *Star Trek* t-shirt.) People may get suspicious if you spend all day every day at your local library trying to spot one. How do you find them?

You have to find your Pips, not to be confused with

peeps. I stole this idea from an old, quirky TV show (I'm embarrassed to admit it), *Ally McBeal.* In this episode, she was told by her stand-up comedian therapist that her distress could be soothed if she found her Pips, as in Gladys Knight and the Pips. Her backup singers. Everybody needs backup singers.

Okay? Let's say that you've taken my advice and found a friend at the Sierra Club meeting, your art class, or the community garden. Let's say that you're now taking Argentine tango lessons and have danced with a few rainforest souls who have friend potential written all over them. Congratulations!

What about those inevitable times when sensitive humans are nowhere to be found? What then? That's when you call on your Pips.

Your Pips aren't actually living people though. They're your spiritual backup singers. They support you when you need it. They remind you that you're loved no matter what. You find them in your imagination, in your heart, in nature, or in your religion.

Maybe you call them guardian angels. Spiritual guides. Trees. Maybe they're the feeling you get when you're hiking in the redwoods. Maybe your Pips are in the night sky.

If you haven't found your Pips yet, check out the actions below.

Remember that finding other rainforest-minded souls isn't easy. Be patient. They're out there. Listen carefully. They're singing your song. Shoo bop shoo bop, my baby, oooooooh.

WHAT YOU CAN DO

1. Write about your experiences of loneliness. What was it like in school when you knew the answers but were ignored by teachers? How did you feel when friends didn't care about your interests and your favorite books? How did you interpret your isolation? What is it like now? Are you still looking for that best friend?

2. Look for activities that appeal to you through Meetup.com. Join an online group such as The School of Life or Intergifted.com. Start your own Meetup group, silent book club, book group, astronomical society, or online community.

3. Admit that you have a rainforest mind, and then do things you love. Use your intuition to spot other rainforest-minded souls while you are there. Take the risk and ask one to tea. She or he will be grateful. You will have a potential friend.

4. Learn the Argentine tango.

5. Get out into nature. Feel the energies of the spirits of the earth. Build a relationship with them. If you need help with this, look into participating in a quest like the ones at Animas Institute.

6. Write in your journal, and begin a dialogue with your Pips. You can find ideas in Christina Baldwin's *Life's Companion: Journal Writing as Spiritual Quest.*

7. Take a class on developing your intuition.

8. Start a meditation practice. Over time, your Pips may show up spontaneously.

9. Read about guided imagery, and use CDs and books by healthjourneys.com that teach you how to use visualization for healing and finding an inner advisor—your own spiritual wisdom.

10. Imagine your Pips. Your spiritual support network singing and dancing right behind you. Melodies. Harmonies. Shoo bop shoo bop. Maybe they look like people. Maybe animals. Maybe shining balls of light. No matter. They are yours. They'll be there when the humans aren't. Don't take my word for it; say you heard it through the grapevine.

11. Therapy can help you face your fears of partnership. In the therapeutic relationship, you practice trusting someone and being vulnerable. You learn how to speak your truth and repair your broken heart. You develop healthy boundaries and shift patterns and beliefs that no longer serve you well. You build self-confidence and self-love so

you are better able to select someone who will be a good match.

12. Explore your psyche to look for obstacles to intimacy and partnership. You may think you want to find someone, but your unconscious may be screaming *"Hell no!"* In your journal, explore your fears. Write to parts of yourself, and be an empathetic listener. Maybe it is your Wounded Child who is afraid of abandonment. Maybe it is your Perfectionist who is afraid of failure. Maybe it is your Introvert who is afraid of being overwhelmed. Write to these parts, and build connections. Find ways to soothe and reassure them. Get yourself out into the world in ways that you find meaningful and fulfilling.

13. Use your creativity to energetically call a partner to you. You can use song writing, collage, letter writing, poetry, dance, painting, gardening, or whatever form works for you and is fun. Imagine that she or he will hear you when the time is right. Imagine what it will feel like when they arrive. Picture your first date. If that image stirs up anxiety, go back to steps one and two! If it creates excitement, that's a good sign. Be like the Buddha, and let go of attachment to outcome. Live your already beautiful, multifaceted, rainforest-minded life.

CHAPTER 10

Mortified by Mediocrity

Many assumptions are made about "smart people." It's important to see what is actually true. Often there is a sense of being an impostor and that if people knew the real you, they would realize you are not as smart as they think you are. Those fears of being found out as a fraud are often coupled with deep fears of failure or being seen as average or mediocre. Efforts to excel can be misread as arrogance. You might be terribly disappointed by the human race. Like everything else in the rainforest, it is complicated.

GOODBYE IMPOSTOR SYNDROME, HELLO AUTHENTICITY

If you were an impostor, you wouldn't be worrying that you are an impostor.

There are people we all know who do not worry about this. They firmly believe that they have all the answers and that they are smart. They do not worry that they are impostors. Kind of like a narcissist doesn't worry that he's a narcissist because he's a narcissist.

You, on the other hand, worry. You have the depth, sensitivity, and intelligence to know that there are no easy answers or quick solutions except, maybe, if you're asking, "Should I eat that hot fudge sundae now or later?"

You don't trust that your depth, sensitivity, and intelligence are enough. You don't trust that it means that you're gifted. You imagine that someday the truth will come out, and you'll be exposed as the fraud you truly are.

What if, just for today, you decided that you couldn't waste any more time worrying when the truth will come out, worrying when you'll be exposed? Worrying when you will fail spectacularly?

You have things to do.

What might that be like, saying goodbye to your impostor syndrome?

Maybe you'd have more time to create. Maybe you'd finally start that project that's been calling your name for years. Maybe your children would need less therapy when they got older. Maybe it would bring you closer to your authentic self and your mission here on earth.

Note: Do not panic about the "mission" thing. No pressure. (Well, maybe a little pressure.) Your mission doesn't need to be to end world hunger, although it can be. Your purpose may be to raise compassionate, sensitive, empathetic humans and/or to end the legacy of abuse in your family line. Imagine if everyone on earth did that.

I know saying goodbye will not be easy. The impostor syndrome is tangled and thorny.

I'm just asking you to start the process. Feel into it. Repeat after me: "*I have a rainforest mind. In my own particular, uniquely magnificent way, I am gifted. If I were really an impostor, I wouldn't be worrying that I'm an impostor.*"

Now let's go eat that sundae.

NOBODY LIKES A KNOW-IT-ALL

What did you do when you were in school and you knew all the answers to the questions the teacher was asking?

Did you raise your hand, expecting that you'd be called on? Did you raise your hand expecting the teacher to ignore you? Did you not raise your hand because the other kids would get mad at you? Did you blurt the answer out of frustration or anger or a touch of ADHD? Did you read *Hamlet* for the fifth time? Did you plan the design for a nuclear fusion reactor? Did you stare out the window in despair looking to the crows for consolation?

All you wanted was to learn something new. To be free to be curious and excited. To share big ideas with your peers. You weren't trying to make anyone else look bad. You weren't trying to show how smart you were. You weren't trying to irritate the teacher. All you wanted was to learn something new, but you were ridiculed and rejected. Maybe your teachers told you, *"Nobody likes a know-it-all."*

Ironic, isn't it? When you're often feeling like an impostor? When you know how much you don't know, you're the last one to think that you know it all.

Maybe you were like Taylor Wilson, just trying to correct the outdated information his science teacher was presenting to the class. Eager to talk with someone about "the esoteric behaviors of baryons and mesons." Exploring nuclear fusion on his own while failing science in school.

Granted, in school, it's hard for teachers to manage large groups of energetic kids and meet each child's particular educational needs. We know this. We need to work to change the system, but for now, and from now on, I don't want you to be blamed for your ravenous hunger for knowledge. I don't want you to be mislabeled. I don't want you to blame yourself.

You're not a know-it-all.

You're a want-to-know-it-all.

WHEN HUMANS KEEP LETTING YOU DOWN

Humans disappoint you. They don't live up to your expectations. Sure, you have high standards, but you're not asking all that much, right? If people just tried harder, they could accomplish a lot. Couldn't they?

Not just relatives and friends. Not just politicians

and educators, but others. Contractors, Internet providers, artists, activists, doctors, celebrities, and psychotherapists. Disappointing. What is wrong with humans? Don't they care about quality? Excellence? Compassion?

Now, I don't know all humans, but I'm guessing that most of them do care. That said, here are some things that you need to know.

When you have a rainforest mind, you have many abilities, a large capacity for learning, and a love of knowledge. You may know a lot in multiple fields, sometimes more than the "experts." You can have exceptionally high standards for your work. Producing quality is part of your identity. Being fair and compassionate matters to you, and all of this feels normal. *Isn't everyone like this?*

No. Everyone is not like this.

You may not have any training in home building, but you may know that your contractor's plan for your family room will not work. You may not have a medical degree, but you may know that your cardiologist is not seeing the whole picture. You have never run a nonprofit, but in two weeks, you could set up a system that would provide much greater efficiency and productivity. You may not have a psychology degree, but you're a better counselor than your psychotherapy-trained coworkers.

People tell you that you expect too much. That you need to be satisfied with less. That mediocrity is good enough. That you're an overachiever and an arrogant know-it-all. That you need to "shut up and sing" (to quote a powerful song by the Dixie Chicks).

These messages and experiences can make you feel a little crazy, a little less than. Maybe a lot less than. Lonely. Too responsible.

You may wonder how to live your best life when people you'd like to depend upon keep dropping the ball. You're tired of always picking up the balls. So darned many balls.

Your family, your community, and your world need you. Your excellence. Your quality. Your compassion. Now more than ever.

So you can still sing. Definitely sing.

But don't shut up.

ARE YOU TOO SMART TO FAIL?

You don't like to fail. In fact, you may be terrified of failure, and you have trouble not seeing any minor mistake as a monumental failure. Right? Am I in your head? Yeah? It's pretty wild in here. So many monkeys.

What is failure? What are the advantages of failure? Why do I think you should start failing as soon as you can, especially if you're a parent?

Just so we're clear, I'm not suggesting that you begin to fail as in become a serial killer. Start a cocaine habit. Forget to pick your kids up at school for several days. Just so we're clear.

You weren't born afraid to fail. Watch a child learning to walk. Lots of failing. Early learning includes much trial and much error. When did you become too

Paula Prober

big to fail? Now, do you worry that you're too smart to fail?

If you were a fast learner, if you were an early reader, if you used words like "entomology" when you were five, if you were told over and over how smart you were, if there were piles of praise every time you aced a test, you may have felt that your abilities and achievements were what made you worthy, what made you lovable. You may have concluded that anything less than perfect was a failure, and failure meant that you were not such a smart person after all.

It's time to start failing.

You don't have to fail like Elon Musk and blow up a rocket. You don't have to fail like Steve Jobs and be fired from the company you created. Small "failures" will be fine for starters. Excellence instead of perfection, for example. A grade of B on your final exam. A loud emotional outburst in the middle of a board meeting.

Eventually, you may even rethink the word failure. Instead, you'll make a mistake, an error, a gaffe, a blunder. Small stuff. No big deal. Even if you experience an actual failure, you'll know it's something that you *do*, not something that you *are*.

Trust me. You'll still be smart. You'll still be lovable, and you will learn much more from failure than you'll ever learn from success. Your children will thank you.

And your stand-up comedy routines? They'll be so much funnier.

WHAT YOU CAN DO

1. Do you grapple with impostor syndrome? If you do, join the club. I'm not sure I know any rainforest-minded soul who doesn't. It can get pretty complex, so I'm going to recommend *The Secret Thoughts of Successful Women* by Valerie Young. Sorry, fellas. They say it's more common among women, but I know you feel it, too.

2. Notice when you start to feel like an impostor. In what situations? At what times? Start keeping track. Write about it. Imagine that the impostor is a part of you but not all of you. It's a subpersonality that wants to protect you. From what? Start a dialogue with the impostor; see what it's trying to do and what it needs to calm down.

3. You may be feeling major frustration with humans right now. There is so much suffering. You may not know where to begin. Write about your disappointment. Give yourself permission to feel your sadness, frustration, and anger. Writing about it can give you clarity around the depth of your feelings and what actions you can take. When you need something uplifting, go to YouTube and find Lin Manuel-Miranda's song to his wife at their wedding.

4. Start to keep track of your failures and mistakes and how they changed things for the better. This will be useful when you write your memoir.

CHAPTER 11

Social Responsibility and Your Bad Hair Days

A rainforest mind often comes with a sense of responsibility for creating a better world, a desire to make a difference. It may or may not come from pressure to use your gift or reach your potential. I often see it as an innate drive to contribute. In times of great turmoil, such as these, it can be easy to fall into despair. You may ask, *"What can one person do?"* Let me help you find out.

CHANGE THE WORLD

We stand on the threshold of a great unknown. Individually and collectively, we launch into an uncertain future—at once, both perilous and saturated with possibility. Our accustomed, culturally-determined roles and identities are inadequate to navigate the sea change of our time. Our collective journey requires a radical shift in the human relationship with the community of all life—a cultural transformation so profound that future humans might regard it as an evolution of consciousness. Safe passage requires each of us to offer our full magnificence to the world.

—Bill Plotkin, Animas Valley Institute

How do you offer your "full magnificence" to the world? Because now would be a great time to do such a thing. Don't you agree?

I have a few ideas.

You have to believe that you have magnificence.

Yes, I know that won't be easy. Maybe it feels impossible, but I know that you've got it. I'm sure of it. Somewhere, buried deep inside, you know it too. You'll need to find a way to dive into your heart or into your soul or into wherever your magnificence lives and touch it. Gently. Tenderly.

All you need is to get a glimpse of it. For starters. A teensy weensy glimpse.

Perhaps you can find it through yoga, mindfulness practices, painting, dancing, music, acupuncture, martial arts, excursions in nature, prayer, shamanic journeying, poetry, journaling, reading, gazing at the night sky, Reiki, running, watching your child sleep, psychotherapy, bungee jumping, or some combination of these or other things.

It could take a while, but it'll be worth it. Trust me on this.

Once you get a teensy weensy glimpse, you'll want to expand your connection. To do this, you'll need to understand that your magnificence is something you *are*, not something you *do*. Recognizing your magnificence is not the same as conceit, arrogance, self-centeredness, or grandiosity. It's the opposite. It's finding that place within you that's all about love. Love and compassion. Love for yourself, your mistakes, your failures, your successes, your disabilities, your persnicketiness, your idealism, your sensitivities, your intuitions, your over-excitability, your obsessions, your perfectionism, your loneliness, and your bad hair days.

Love for your family, your community, your world, and your planet.

I know. I'm asking a lot.

If you grew up in a dysfunctional family with chain saw relatives, for example, you might feel less than magnificent.

If you were bullied in school or teased for being *too sensitive* or *too curious* or *too everything*, you might feel less than magnificent.

If you don't fit into the "acceptable" ethnic group, race, sexual orientation, body size, religion, personality, or age, you might feel less than magnificent.

But I know the truth, and you will too.

Once you've met and believe in your magnificence. I'm betting that it will tell you how to share it with the world. And, then, you will change it.

IF YOU ARE GIFTED, ARE YOU RESPONSIBLE FOR EVERYONE AND EVERYTHING UNTIL THE END OF TIME?

The following questions can plague the rainforest minded.

- If someone asks you for help, and you have the skills that they need, are you always supposed to say yes to them?

- If someone asks you for help, and you have the skills that they need and you say no, should you feel utterly and totally guilty for the rest of your life?

- If your intuition is often accurate, and you pick up information about someone, are you responsible for telling that person what you suspect is true about them?

- If you can see into someone's wounded soul, and you have compassion for them, but in everyday life they're toxic, manipulating creeps, do you have to keep being their friend?

There are many other questions, of course, bazillions of them, but the above questions are in a particular category: *If I'm gifted, I must be responsible for using my gifts to the fullest capacity possible all the time.*

That category. You've probably heard this all of your life from relatives, teachers, religious leaders, and yourself. I get it. It makes sense that you should develop your gifts, that you want to be of service. That you feel a drive to make a difference. To use your superpowers for good.

It's why I write this blog. I'm driven to be of service to *you* so that you can rediscover your strength and your confidence and walk your many paths to self-actualization, human evolution, and planetary healing, but there are limits.

Yes, even you. have. limits.

For example, you have a body that you must take care of. You need to sleep. Your sensitivity and empathy need to be protected and nourished. There's only so much time.

If you grew up in a chain saw family, you'll have a child part who learned that they had to be perfect or risk abandonment or annihilation. That child will need your attention, understanding, and love.

Here are some other things that you may need to learn:

You'll want to learn the difference between obsession with and excitement over a new project that is so intellectually stimulating that you forget to eat or bathe for days on end. (Yeah.)

Versus:

When you are responding to just one more email from your clamoring friend or coworker who just has one last tiny request that you design, write, and print the programs for their long-lost fourth cousin's memorial gathering and you edit the eulogy and order the flowers after you bake your nephew's favorite cheesecake and don't forget that it has to be gluten-free and bring your violin to the service just in case and you don't have time to eat or bathe for days on end. (Nah.)

Not only that.

You'll want to learn that you can't possibly say yes to every request that you get even if you could do it faster and better than anyone else available. Just because you are able to do it doesn't mean you have to. It would be impossible to do everything that you can do. You will have to say *no* some of the time.

You'll want to learn that you have a right to select your friends carefully. If you find yourself doing all the listening and supporting, you may need to say bye-bye. If you always feel drained or weird after visiting, bid them adieu.

You may have highly developed intuitive abilities. This is particularly tricky. When do you share what you know? How do you protect yourself from people with terrible boundaries who will never get enough no matter how much you give? You need to set the boundaries when they don't. Use that intuition of yours to know when and how much to share. You have a right to protect your intuitive/spiritual self from assault.

Do you hear me?

Sure. You will likely want to create a life of meaning, purpose, and service. You may even be heading toward self-actualization, human evolution, and planetary healing as we speak.

Just remember that even though you're gifted, you're not responsible for everyone and everything until the end of time.

I mean it.

SPIRITUAL INTELLIGENCE

Being the super sensitive, emotional, deeply aware human that you are, I suspect that you're feeling a bit discombobulated these days. Okay. Extremely distressed and anxious these days. From where I sit in North America, there's a lot to be discombobulated (read: extremely distressed and anxious) about. A lot. You may be overwhelmed with grief, rage, or despair. You may feel a responsibility to act but not know your best path. You may feel pressure to be brilliant because, after all, you're *so smart*.

I want to send you some extra love and inspiration.

To do that, I need to step into more iffy territory. Some of you may balk, but these times require risk, expansion, and iffy territory.

Are you with me?

Okay then.

Here's the overall plan: Believe in your deeply introspective journey. It will heal you and inform your outer action. (If your journey includes psychotherapy, thank you for your courage.) Explore your spirituality. Imagine that you can access guidance from a powerful, loving energy both inside you and around you. Tap into this energy in nature and in what might be called the invisible world or, as I like to call it, the Force. Use the techniques that sing to you such as meditation, poetry, dancing, gardening, art making, blogging, praying, journaling, yoga, religion, dreaming, camping, hiking, traveling, studying, drumming, or journeying. In this way, find your version of a spiritual intelligence that will move you closer to your greater purpose. Then you will know what actions to take.

Got it?

Here's some inspiration from mythologist Martin Shaw's article on Medium, *A Counsel of Resistance and Delight in the Face of Fear*:

When the lots are counted, when we are gathered in, we will find that it was love that mattered. Love expressed, given, received, fought for. So for those of us fighting right now, I say; keep going. As a culture, as an individual, believe in the full life that is your bequeathed inheritance, not the subterranean half-life that terror and impoverished minded bullies will try and spike your wine with. You are too good for that...Wander your oak valleys, linger in ornate chapels at dusk, get thrown out of the tavern at midnight, be kind, kiss the wounded, fight injustice and protect, protect, protect all the trembling bells of delight that you notice out of the corner of your eye when every-one else is oblivious. Value yourself, know yourself, don't be naive, but don't be afraid of love. Carry it.

From psychologist Kathleen D. Noble in *Riding the Windhorse*:

We are never truly alone. Not only does there exist an immense network of intelligent and loving allies who sustain and support us as we struggle to grow, but also some portion of our larger self always comprehends what we are doing and where we are heading. No matter where we might find ourselves in the vast complexity of the whole, there is always a level of awareness that is old enough and smart enough to understand…each of us, no matter how small or insignificant we might sometimes feel, is vital to the whole, to a depth and degree we are wont to forget.

From *Star Wars*:

"May the Force be with you."

WHAT YOU CAN DO

1. Write out your feelings about the present state of the world. Are you feeling overwhelmed? Powerless? Angry? It can help to release these feelings into a journal or a piece of art. Instead of repressing the despair, if you move into it and acknowledge it deeply, you might find creative resources underneath and a sense of what you can do next.

2. In the internal family systems model, you are a compilation of subpersonalities with a higher Self at your center. Rather than being the total impostor-slacker-anxiety-ridden lost soul that you may see in your mirror on occasion, you are a human with many parts and a deep, authentic, radiant essence at your core. You might have an inner critic, a wounded child, a scared addict, or a paralyzed perfectionist on your list of subpersonalities. Be fair; you may also have an artist, healer, empath, scholar, inventor, athlete, and nature lover in your psyche. What do you do? Read on.

3. In your journal, enumerate your many parts. Choose one, and start a dialogue. The idea is that you can converse with and get to know all aspects of yourself. In this way, you become

friends with your shadow and learn what it can teach you. You invigorate the parts that are your strengths. You begin to connect with the authentic, radiant Self at your core. With this, you become more empowered to make a difference.

4. You may have searched for a mentor, someone to guide you as you look for your purpose on the planet. Make a list of humans you admire. Perhaps they're authors, poets, scientists, artists, musicians, ancestors, or athletes. They don't have to be living. You don't have to have met them. They can include animal companions or spiritual guides. Select about five to be your mentors, your committee, or your backup singers. List their names and what each one has to offer you. Maybe it's support for your creative project. Maybe it's a sense of humor. Maybe it's a hug when you're in despair. Write to them when you need help. Ask for guidance. Visualize yourself receiving their assistance, or write the response in a letter from them. You may be pleasantly surprised at the results.

5. Take a quiet moment, and create an image of your Wise Self (some people call it their Future Self). Write and/or draw them in detail. Feel into them deeply with all your senses. Picture them standing in front of you. What do they have

to tell you? Step into them, and feel that Wise Self in your body. Breathe slowly, and deepen your connection. Use all your senses. Stay with the feeling, and notice if they have any more messages for you. Know that you can reconnect with your Wise Self at any time. It will get easier with practice.

CHAPTER 12

My Smart Kid Is So Emotional— Am I a Parenting Failure?

If you have a rainforest mind and are a parent, chances are good that you'll have a gifted child. Because you are likely to have similar rainforest-y characteristics and because of the complexities of the rainforest, raising this child could be somewhat (or very) challenging. People will tell you that you are so lucky to have such a smart child. You may not feel lucky, but it is hard to find other parents who understand why you feel overwhelmed, exhausted, and lonely.

If your child is like you, you may find yourself easily triggered by extreme emotional responses or schooling challenges. It might be hard for you to remain calm if your nervous system is easily activated. If you experienced early trauma and haven't addressed it via a therapeutic process, you may find yourself repeating patterns from your family of origin. The more you understand your deep beliefs, patterns, and behaviors and address the unresolved pain from your past, the better you will be at providing a healthy, loving environment for your child.

THE WORST PARENT EVER

Your child is emotional. Anxious. Melting down. Telling you that you are the worst parent. Ever. Not in so many words necessarily, but still. You know that you are the worst parent. Ever.

How can such a smart kid behave this way? you wonder. *How did I screw up so badly?*

I hear this often from parents of gifted children. Here's what I tell them.

1. Gifted kids are *emotional.* Their passionate natures can be as large as their intellects. You can respect their emotions while setting boundaries around inappropriate behavior. They will be calmer if they know that you are compassionate *and* in charge.

2. Helping your children contain emotion is different from repressing or denying those feelings. Containment is useful, especially when you're in public places where screeching will be frowned upon. They can visualize a beautiful object, a tree, a coconut, or whatever their creative minds can dream up that will lovingly hold their emotions when it's inappropriate to let them flail about.

3. Because smart kids are very perceptive, little things that others don't notice will affect them.

That includes the sound of people chewing or the scent of your detergent. They're not neurotic. They're sensitive. They'll also be finely tuned in to you. They'll know when you're worrying about their grades and pretending that you're not. It's often best to confess the truth.

4. If we're talking about fifteen-year-old (more or less) girls and their moms, don't ignore the awesome power of hormones. Let us all give hormones our utmost respect. They will win every time. Sometimes all you can do is ride the wave, or go read a good book (or visit your naturopath, acupuncturist, or doctor).

5. Recognize when you start channeling your parents. This is not usually helpful. If you find that your mother's criticism is coming out of your mouth or your father's anger is simmering below the surface, consider psychotherapy. A good therapist can help you dig your own voice out from under the rubble.

6. Avoiding power struggles will be hard if your children think faster than you do. Use the *"let me think about it, and I'll get back to you"* method. Give yourself time to make decisions so you don't feel pressured. It'll be easier for everyone to stay calm—including you. Remember that your child will feel safer if you're in charge.

7. You may be a problem solver and action oriented. When your children are in pain, it's hard to not want to stop the pain immediately. Instead, start listening. Reflect back what you hear. Validate feelings. Ask them if they want your help problem solving. If you're listening well, they can often come up with their own solutions. At first, this may feel awkward and contrived. Explain to your kids what you're trying to do, and they'll be patient with you. You may think that you're already listening and it's not working. Ask your children if they think you're listening, and believe them when they tell you that you aren't. (That said, set limits on how long you listen if your child tends to go on and on and on.)

8. If your own childhood was less than ideal, you might lose patience when your child is freaking out, especially if you were never allowed to complain, cry, or fall apart. Give yourself some grace around your reactivity. Find a way to allow the child *in you* to express herself or himself. A journal can be a great way to safely complain, cry, or fall apart. If you need more help, look for good resources online, or seek out your friendly local psychotherapist.

9. There are no perfect parents. Your mistakes are an opportunity to show your child how to learn from mistakes, how to understand that a mistake

is not the same as a failure, and that even failure is an opportunity for growth.

Your child is emotional. Anxious. Melting down. Gifted. So are you.

YOUR GIFTED KID WAS SO ADORABLE

Your daughter, Jenny, is editor of the school newspaper. She's a math whiz, a voracious reader, and a star athlete. At fifteen, she looks destined for a great life.

Why is she freaking out over what looks like nothing? Why is she still having meltdowns? Why is she screeching at you about your fundamentally inadequate parenting?

She was so darned cute when she was three.

Now, school is a struggle. She questions her teachers' authority and refuses to turn in assignments that aren't up to her standards. She criticizes the values of her so-called friends. Even though she has great empathy for the suffering multitudes, there's no empathy for you. None. Nada. Zilch.

Welcome to adolescence. Welcome to GiftedKid 2.0.

I'm exaggerating a little. In fact, she does have empathy for you. Believe it or not, she feels guilty for her outbursts and hides a pressing need to please you. She worries that she's a disappointment and that she'll never live up to your expectations (or her own). Her burning need for intellectual stimulation and her loneliness at not being deeply seen trigger her emotional reactivity.

Not to mention, um, hormones.

Of course, your teen may not be like this at all. Gifted kids come in all shapes, sizes, and varieties, but if you relate to the above, you're not alone.

What can you do besides escape to a deserted island until she's twenty-one? See the exercises below and remember, in the words of Andrew Solomon, "Like parents of children who are severely challenged, parents of exceptionally talented children are custodians of children beyond their comprehension."

YOUR GIFTED CHILD AND SCHOOL

Eight-year-old Bobby wanted to be Richard Feynman for Halloween.

Could he be gifted? Hm?

There were many other signs: enormous enthusiasm for learning, especially history, science, and language; emotional intensity, difficulty maintaining friendships with children his age, trouble with motivation in school, writing insightful poetry and detailed stories, stacks of books he longed to read, advanced verbal ability, overthinking tests so that he misunderstood simple problems and scored poorly on exams, great interest in mathematics but not arithmetic, high sensitivity and empathy, frustration with the slowness of handwriting, distressed by the repetition in school, extremely active and curious mind, and a quirky sense of humor.

I've known many gifted children with similar characteristics. Like Bobby, they're often misunderstood. Their sensitivity and big emotions are mistaken for immaturity. Mediocre test scores are interpreted as average ability or laziness. Loneliness is seen as lack of empathy. Intense curiosity looks like arrogance.

School personnel didn't recognize Bobby's rainforest mind. Is this scenario familiar? If so, here's what you can do.

- Explain to your child what it means to have a rainforest mind.

- Ask your child to create an imaginary container for their emotions to use when it's not safe to express them in public. (Bobby used a coconut reinforced with diamonds that was "*as big as a truck.*") One resource for helping with anxiety, depression, and intensities is Charlotte Reznick's work.

- Find a specialist in gifted education who can test your child if the school needs proof of giftedness so that your child's anxiety and creativity will be taken into consideration as their test results are interpreted.

- Request persistently and repeatedly that your child be matched with the more sensitive, creative, and flexible teachers who have training in gifted education. Did I mention be persistent?

Paula Prober

Convince administrators that this is an easy solution, because it is. Understand the pressures that educators are under, and provide support where you can. Bring caffeinated beverages to overworked teachers. Let difficult administrators know that you have superpowers, and you're not afraid to use them. Remind yourself that when you speak out for your child, other gifted kids will benefit.

- Teach your child social skills, if needed, through role-playing. Rainforest-y kids can be bossy and impatient, because they don't realize that other children don't think as fast or have the same interests. (Explain this to them.) Invite children over for play dates, and provide guidance if needed.

- Problem solve as a family. Brainstorm ideas. Your children will come up with creative solutions to assorted problems, and they'll appreciate your trust in them. Remember that healthy limits and consistency are important, especially if your child is testing boundaries. Take time to nourish yourself.

- If you have a rainforest mind and had difficulty in school, find ways to process your feelings through journaling, coaching, or counseling.

- Read about what other parents are doing and,

if needed, look into homeschooling. Join a parenting support group in your town or on Facebook. Attend a conference with Supporting the Emotional Needs of the Gifted or the National Association for Gifted Children.

- Work to change the system. Join innovative educators like those at NuMinds and organizations like 4pt0.org.

All of our children—in fact, the entire planet—will benefit if our gifted kids are provided with a stimulating, compassionate, meaningful schooling experience.

I'm sure Richard Feynman would agree.

IMAGINE A WORLD WHERE GIFTED KIDS DON'T HAVE TO WAIT

It all started in first grade when you eagerly finished the entire workbook in one night. You thought your teacher would be pleased. She was not pleased. You were told to sit and color the pictures and *wait* until the other first graders caught up with you.

There was the time they were teaching addition, and you had been doing complicated calculations in your head since you were four. You were told to *wait*. You were too young to learn fractions.

When you were eleven, you were dying to read *The Autobiography of Malcolm X,* but you were told to *wait.* That was the book everyone was required to read in high school.

When you scored in the ninety-ninth percentile in reading and math and could easily work two years above grade level, it was decided that you shouldn't skip a grade. You needed to *wait* until you were more emotionally and socially mature, even though you were capable of contributing confidently to discussions with your parents' friends.

You wanted to know about death and God. You were told to *wait* until you were a grown-up, because you wouldn't understand.

You are still waiting.

Your colleagues at work take hours to conclude what you knew last week.

Your boss wants you to calm down and slow down and not share your ideas just yet. Maybe next week.

You completed all your assigned work for the day, and it's only 1:00 pm.

Your supervisor says she'll get back to you with the answers to your questions. She never does.

You've learned everything you can about your job, and now the tasks are frustrating and boring.

You wonder when you can share the fascinating article you read in *The New Yorker* while friends talk about recipes and reality TV.

You have so much to say about so many things, but you have to find the right time to speak so that you don't overwhelm your partner, friends, relatives, children, and pets with your enthusiasm, sensitivities, and ideas.

(Okay, maybe your pets aren't overwhelmed.)

Waiting. Waiting. Waiting.

In *The Boy Who Played with Fusion*, Tom Clynes wrote, "*Waiting* was the most common response when Tracy Cross of the college of William and Mary asked thirteen thousand kids in seven states to describe in one word their experience as gifted children."

Thirteen thousand kids. Waiting.

Imagine a world where gifted kids don't have to wait. A world where you can be yourself. Imagine the possibilities.

I want to live in that world.

EXISTENTIAL DEPRESSION IN TEENS

Beth came to see me for counseling when she was sixteen. Unlike many teens who might be reluctant to seek counseling, she asked her mother to find her a therapist. She knew she was in trouble. When her mom contacted me, she said that Beth used to be energetic, motivated, athletic, and a high achiever in school. When she was nine, she planned her future: running for president of the United States.

Lately, she'd become depressed and lethargic. Her grades were dropping. Life had become pointless. What happened?

Beth told me that she was lonely. Her one friend, Maddie, was unreliable, using Beth as her counselor but never reciprocating. Beth said that kids her age weren't interested in politics or philosophy. They weren't asking existential questions. For Beth, finding a boyfriend always ended up in disappointment. The boys would accuse her of overthinking or being too serious. School was disappointing as well. In one instance, she said that she'd read *1984* in English class and spent hours analyzing the implications of the book and rewriting her essays. Her classmates dismissed the book, saying it was "*stupid.*"

Beth was a worrier. She was searching for meaning in her life and the world at large. She questioned everything: the importance of grades, whether college would be worth the money, her "*laziness,*" Internet censorship, GMOs, how she would find a meaningful career, the "*enormity of the universe,*" how to deal with climate change, and on and on.

Yet Beth didn't know that she was gifted. Even though she scored well on tests, she didn't see herself as particularly smart. She hadn't been identified as gifted in school. She didn't see that her problems were related to her rainforest mind.

I explained it to her.

I told her that she fit the profile to a *t*: extreme curiosity, constant questioning, intense sensitivity, loneliness, unusual empathy, perfectionism, intuition, passion for learning, multiple interests and abilities, anxiety, and existential depression. Yep. Rainforest mind.

It took a while to convince her. She said that she was "*average*" and didn't want to seem critical of others or ungrateful. Eventually, she believed me. She wasn't a freak or lazy or a misfit. She was gifted. Now that she knew who she was and what to look for, she could find intellectual peers and look for people and organizations that also wanted to change the world. She could accept that these rainforest-y traits were positive qualities. She could research many career paths and build a life that mattered.

Perhaps she'd decide to run for president after all.

WHAT YOU CAN DO

1. Make a list of your frustrations and fears. It can help to acknowledge your anxieties rather than deny them and expect yourself to be perfect. You may excel at many things but not feel competent at the parenting gig. Know that you won't damage your child beyond repair if you make mistakes. Write a list of affirmations that you can repeat to yourself in tough times. (For example: "*My mistakes will teach my children that they don't have to be perfect.*")

2. Make a list of self-care activities. Include ways to get intellectual stimulation. Take time away from your children to nourish yourself.

3. Remind yourself that overexcitabilities (OEs) are part of the rainforest-minded package. Gifted kids are emotionally and intellectually more intense. To find out more about OEs, read Daniels' *Living with Intensity.*

4. Try your best not to take the criticism personally. This is not easy. Breathe. Learn to meditate. Get exercise.

5. Listen and reflect your child's feelings during the emotional turmoil. Problem solve later. No advice. No criticism. Listening is key. It's a simple

idea but not easy to do.

6. Read Eileen Kennedy-Moore's *Smart Parenting for Smart Kids* and my book, *Your Rainforest Mind: A Guide to the Well-Being of Gifted Adults and Youth*.

7. If you are repeating patterns from your childhood and are still not in therapy, start looking for a counselor who has a background in working with rainforest minds. It will be the best thing you can do for your child.

CHAPTER 13

If I'm So Smart, Why Do I Need Psychotherapy?

This entire book is useful as a guide for therapists and their clients. That said, there are therapy-related ideas that are important to note separately. Not all therapists come from the same theoretical perspective. My bias is that it is important to process the experiences in your family of origin. For the rainforest-minded in particular, it seems that a depth approach works well. In my experience, it is likely that you won't be satisfied with symptom relief. You will need to understand the source of your pain and go to the root. You will respond well to a longer, deeper approach that intends to heal and transform. It takes courage to embark on the therapy journey, but you and everyone you know—even people you don't know—will benefit.

PATH TO A BETTER WORLD

Things are looking kinda crazy these days. It's hard to know what to think, what to do, or how to be. There are so many issues worldwide that need attention. What should super sensitive, empathetic, insightful, emotional humans do?

Well, being the obsessed-with-psychotherapy psychotherapist that I am, you can guess what I'm about to say. Hang in there with me.

What if you start with yourself and your family? What if you take some time to examine your own fears, doubts, and despair? What if you take a trip into your past to understand the legacy your dysfunctional family handed you? Locate your true self, and pull her or him out from under the rubble. If all humans would recover the self-acceptance, compassion, and creativity that was smooshed or buried or broken or clobbered during those early years, might we create a path to a better world?

Heck yeah.

I know that what I'm asking isn't easy. It takes great courage to make this journey. *Don't let anyone tell you otherwise.* In case you're wondering, examining the multiple ways you were clobbered isn't about blaming your parents willy-nilly, irreverently dismantling the lovely coping strategies you've so cleverly designed, or slashing open old wounds so that you bleed for years all over your so-impractical white sofa. No. It's not that.

It is about understanding what happened so that you can put the puzzle pieces together and answer the questions that have plagued you for years. Questions about your fears and doubts and despair. Questions like these: *If I'm so smart, why am I scared all the time? If I'm so smart, why are my relationships so difficult? If I'm so smart, why do I feel like a worthless crazy catastrophizing ne'er-do-well?*

You may say, *But I do understand what happened, and that hasn't changed anything.* I know. That's because it's not just about intellectual understanding, although that's the place to start. It's also about a safe, supported grieving process. An opportunity to process the sadness, anger, shame, and regret that live in your broken heart. An opportunity to find and love those child parts of you that have been abandoned and trampled.

By the way, this is a big deal.

How big? You're stopping the legacy of dysfunction in your family line, handed down through generations. The dysfunction stops with you. That big.

Not only that. In a deep therapeutic process, you're healing your portion of the psychospiritual web. We're all connected, so it's not just your family line. It's all of us.

I mean it.

Just when you thought that was enough, there's more. I am not making this up. Along with the sweet child parts that you rescue from the abyss, you will be astonished by spurts of creativity and sparks of intuition (the voice of your true Self!). Expansion of your softened heart. An even greater compassion for others. Energy and inspiration.

There's your path. Better world?

Indeed.

DIVING INTO THE ABYSS

What happens to your sensitivity, empathy, and intellect when you grow up in a seriously dysfunctional family? How does your perceptive mind and open heart survive the alcoholic parent or the emotional abuse? What beliefs or patterns set up in your childhood follow you into adulthood? When is it time to find a good psychotherapist and dive into the abyss?

In this post, I'll begin to answer these questions. Disclaimer: I'm speaking only to my experience with my particular clients and myself. Okay? I don't speak for all psychotherapy everywhere (but you knew that).

Here's what I see. Even though you're supersensitive, emotional, and aware that you can be easily hurt, you're also terribly resilient because you're super sensitive, emotional, and aware. You're likely affected if you grew up in a chain saw family system, and yet there's something gorgeous-powerful deep inside you that was untouched. Your self-esteem is what's been damaged. You have a distorted sense of your true Self. That may look like lack of self-confidence, getting into abusive relationships, self-hatred, underachieving, anxiety, and depression.

As a child, you were so vulnerable that you had to believe what your parents told you. It was inevitable that you'd misinterpret their dysfunction to mean that something was wrong with you. Even though you were smart, the intensity of parental shame, fear, rage, and who knows what got transmitted to you. This is what needs to be dismantled: your misunderstanding of who you are.

That requires diving into the abyss. Poet Adrienne Rich calls it *Diving into the Wreck.*

Yeah. Abyss. Wreck. Oh boy. You'll want a guide. Someone who's been in their own abyss and is familiar with it. Someone who has explored their wreck and found the buried treasure hidden inside.

It can be a scary proposition. It can take time. Even though you're a fast learner, this process is slow. You'll get impatient and think you're doing it wrong. You'll have times when you feel overwhelming sadness. You'll wonder why the hell you thought that hanging out in an abyss was such a grand idea.

Eventually you'll find that it's worth the time, money, and tears. You'll notice changes in your inner and outer worlds. You'll start to discover your gorgeous-powerful self.

That doesn't mean that the wreck will disappear, by the way. You may fall in every now and then. Get lost. Flounder. Cry. Shriek. It'll be less scary, more familiar, smaller. You'll add a cozy chair or hang a piece of art.

While you're there, well, you'll find the jewels.

WHAT PSYCHOTHERAPISTS NEED TO KNOW ABOUT GIFTED CLIENTS

If you are a counselor or other mental health practitioner or if you're gifted and want to see a psychotherapist, there are some things you need to know.

The rainforest mind is complicated. Like the jungle, it's breathtaking in its capacity to create thoughts, emotions, questions, sensitivities, worries, beauty, and iPhones. It's intense and overwhelming. The rainforest mind in counseling needs deep, empathetic, authentic understanding of its fascinating and convoluted intricacies.

Your counselor will need to recognize how you are different. Here are some clues a practitioner can use. A gifted adult may have any or all of the following:

❑ Advanced vocabulary, existential questions and concerns from an early age, multiple in-depth interests

❑ A range of deeper-than-normal emotions and sensitivities (often underground in men), advanced analytical abilities, need for precision in fields of interest, perfectionism, rapid thinking, talking, and learning

❑ Excessive worry, great empathy for all living things, unusual insight into oneself

❑ Avid reading, unending curiosity, and passion for learning (not necessarily for schooling)

❑ More complex ethical, moral, and justice concerns, insight about things that others don't notice, tendency to argue for fun or for intellectual stimulation

❑ Idealism, wit, imagination, creativity, questioning authority and the meaning of life

❑ Loneliness, anxiety (particularly when bored or during extreme bouts of thinking), existential depression, self-doubt even with seeming successes

❑ As a child, difficulty finding friends, serious schooling frustrations, uneven development, or all the above

Once your counselor recognizes your rainforest-mindedness, he or she needs to be able to do the following:

❑ Help you differentiate between struggles caused by giftedness and difficulties caused by other factors.

❑ Be extremely sensitive and authentic.

❑ Create a large container so that you can be as intense and complicated as you are.

❑ Be aware that you might hide your pain and level of trauma through your capacity to achieve, caretaking of others (including your counselor), sense of responsibility, optimism, and idealism.

❑ Understand why you might have been misdiagnosed in the past (giftedness can look like

ADHD, OCD, and even bipolar disorder). Know what it means to be "twice exceptional" (2e).

❏ Acknowledge his or her limits.

❏ Provide parents with strategies and resources for themselves and their children, particularly around the schooling conundrum.

HOW TO FIND A PSYCHOTHERAPIST WHO LOVES YOUR RAINFOREST MIND

How do you find a psychotherapist who isn't over-whelmed by your fast talking, fast thinking, complex emotions, difficult questions, and multiple sensitivities?

How do you find a psychotherapist who isn't fright-ened by your uncanny ability to notice when she or he is distracted or slightly out of whack?

How do you find a psychotherapist who isn't fooled by your articulate insight, wit, and idealism, a psycho-therapist who sees beneath the surface to the deep pain and shame that suffocates you?

How do you find a psychotherapist who knows the difference between giftedness and ADHD, OCD, and bipolar disorder?

How do you find a psychotherapist who can under-stand your long, complicated, nonlinear, out-of-the-box explanations and experiences?

How do you find a psychotherapist who is energized and not drained by your intensity and who gets your sense of humor?

How do you find a psychotherapist who's also been a client and who knows the importance of his or her own continued self-examination?

To understand what you're looking for, ask yourself these questions, and try the suggestions below.

WHAT YOU CAN DO

1. What are your thoughts about therapy? Fear? Anticipation? What would you want to accomplish? What are your goals? Make lists or draw mind maps to sort out your thoughts, fears, and goals.

2. If you've been in therapy before, write about what worked and what didn't. You can take this list to your next therapist.

3. Be willing to shop around for a while until your intuition unequivocally says "yes."

4. Look for a psychotherapist who also has a rainforest mind.

5. Bring relevant articles on giftedness to a first meeting. See how the therapist responds to your request that she or he read up on the topic.

6. Know that you might need to see professionals in different modalities for a more comprehensive approach (body workers, acupuncturists, energy healers, medical doctors, naturopaths, herbalists, etc.).

7. Look for people who are trained in depth psychology (psychodynamic, internal family systems, somatic experiencing, object relations,

Jungian, and others) and feel that it is important to look at your family of origin as part of the healing process.

8. Ask therapists about their own counseling process and how they manage stress and self-care.

9. Know that your therapist will not be perfect. They will occasionally get overwhelmed and out of whack or get lost in your long, complicated, nonlinear, out-of-the-box explanations and experiences. If you are with the right person, they will own up to it. Admit mistakes. Won't stop loving you and your fabulous rainforest mind.

10. If you are in therapy or if you are a therapist, get *Misdiagnosis and Dual Diagnoses of Gifted Children and Adults* by James Webb. Giftedness can look like ADHD, OCD, or bipolar disorder. It's important to know the differences. Some clients will be 2e. They may be rainforest minded along with a disability or another diagnosis. Webb's book is a good way to begin to sort through the complexities.

11. You can find lists of therapists around the world at sengifted.org and hoagiesgifted.org. The School of Life has many excellent articles and videos. They also have therapists who work online.

CHAPTER 14

The Good News

have focused on the many challenges that can exist when you have a rainforest mind. What about all of the good stuff, you might ask? Are there benefits to having a rainforest mind, and if there are, can you acknowledge them and not feel guilty?

One reason you may have been uncomfortable with acknowledging your rainforest mind is that it makes you uncomfortable to think of yourself as smart or smarter than someone else. You don't want to appear arrogant or conceited. It is a tricky place to be to allow yourself to see your strengths and appreciate your achievements while hoping others won't feel less than. I hope that this book will be your safe place to have your whole range of feelings. Here is some of the good news.

THE BENEFITS

I imagine that you experience, on a daily basis, how it's not easy being gifted, but many people assume that it's a perfectly fabulous life of great achievement and private jets that fly you to your second mansion on your personal island paradise every other weekend. Maybe you also believed that and, because your life isn't perfectly fabulous, assumed that you weren't gifted.

It may be hard to speak about your strengths and accomplishments without being seen as arrogant, conceited, or insensitive. Without feeling guilty. That you don't deserve these abilities and achievements. That it was a fluke that you got that award or promotion. It's weird that people keep asking you how you know so much when you know how much you don't know.

How can you identify your strengths, accept them, and be comfortable in your intense, emotional, supersmart, sensitive skin?

For starters, here's my handy dandy list of ways your rainforest mind is beneficial.

- Sensitivity: Makes you a better parent, healer, therapist, colleague, cook, artist, political activist, dancer, musician, teacher, spouse, medical professional, realtor, electrician, plumber, neighbor, everything. You see? Whatever you do, being sensitive makes you better at it. You're perceptive. You notice things others don't. You have deep emotions. You care. Think of it this way: Would you prefer working with a sensitive dentist or an insensitive one?

- Intensity: You're passionate, mysterious, and fascinating. You can get a lot done in a short amount of time. You scare away people you'd rather not talk to anyway.

- Fast, deep, and wide learning, curiosity: The world needs more people who know something, think deeply, ask questions, seek answers, and analyze possibilities. When things get dull, you can always captivate yourself.

- Sense of humor: You are fun to have around in uncomfortable situations. People will overlook your quirks.

- Creativity: Whether it's art, music, inventing, problem solving, designing, filming, synthesizing, rocket launching, brainstorming, writing, parenting, teaching, knitting, or something else, your creating is medicine.

- Perfectionism: You have the intrinsic, driving need to create beauty, harmony, balance, and justice. Everyone benefits from excellence and quality. If you're a surgeon, you're popular.

- Empathy: See sensitivity—it makes you a better everything. You understand and feel the hearts of humans, animals, and plants. You'll probably never start a war.

- Multipotentiality: You can change jobs easily when things get dull. There are countless ways that you are useful. Your children will appreciate how entertaining you are. Your memoir will be a best seller.

- Social conscience: You need to make the world a better place. Because of your sensitivity, intensity, learning capacity, curiosity, sense of humor, creativity, perfectionism, empathy, and multipotentiality, you will make it so.

SO YOU'RE GIFTED. WHO CARES? WHY DOES IT MATTER?

It matters. Even if no one else cares, it matters that you know and that you care.

"Why?" you ask with that quizzical, oh-so-disarming look of yours. (Yes, I know that look.)

Because, my darling:

You will understand that what you imagined were poor communication skills was actually your inability to slow your super-speedy thoughts. Not to mention your assumption that everyone thinks as deeply, quickly, and multidimensionally as you do. They don't. (This does not make them terrible people. I know. It just means that they might not understand your perturbations.)

You will give yourself permission to be the voracious learner that you are. To let yourself dive into the esoteric, obscure, mysterious, complex topics that other people can't possibly grok and wouldn't want to.

You will allow yourself to be obsessed with beauty, balance, harmony, precision, and justice even if it means that you don't get as much done because you're crying over the majesty of the night sky.

You will have compassion and appreciation for your ridiculously high standards and expectations and your need to ruminate over the exact wording of your email to the plumber.

You will understand why you've been lonely all these years and stop thinking it's because you don't smile enough or make small talk or you suck at sports.

You'll find an appropriate career path or two or ten.

You'll protect yourself from the assault of perfumes, ragers, leaf blowers, clamoring hoards, noisy chewers, inconsiderate humans, boring lectures, and houses that are painted orange.

You will understand that what looks quirky, eccentric, weird, and geeky to others is what makes you fascinating.

You will stop misdiagnosing yourself with labels such as OCD, ADHD, bipolar disorder, Asperger's syndrome, lazy, weird, or just plain crazy. (Sure, you may be 2e and have a particular diagnosis along with your rainforest mind, but there's a whole lot of misdiagnosing goin' on, too, so you're gonna stop that now.)

You will appreciate your curiosity and questioning of everything. You'll continue to search for meaning, purpose(s), and justice. This will result in benefits to neighbors, relatives, friends, animals, plants, the planet, and humanity at large.

Let me say that again in a different way.

Knowing that you are gifted matters. It will explain what might otherwise create confusion, self-doubt, anxiety, depression, angst, or despair. It will allow you to blossom into the best human that you can be.

This will result in benefits to neighbors, relatives, friends, animals, plants, the planet, and humanity at large.

Even if they don't know that they care.

THEY SAY YOU'RE A GEEK

They say, *Get realistic, your standards are excessive.* You say, *I need to raise the bar.*

They say, *Slow down and calm down.* You say, *I pump my brakes, but they still can't keep up.*

They say, *You're too sensitive.* You say, *Doesn't everyone cry at an orange-fuchsia-purple-mauve sunset?*

They say, *You're obsessive-compulsive.* You say, *I need to do more research.*

They say, *You're a know-it-all.* You say, *I'm an impostor.*

They say, *You read too much.* You say, *So many books, so little time.*

They say, *You need to pick one career.* You say, *So many careers, so little time.*

They say, *We don't follow your reasoning.* You say, *They just aren't trying hard enough.*

They say, *You shouldn't take things so seriously.* You say, *They need to get out of denial.*

They say, *You're naive for being so optimistic and idealistic.* You say, *They need to dig more deeply.*

They say, *You aren't having any fun.* You say, *It's complicated.*

They say, *You don't finish anything.* You say, *I learned it. I don't need to finish it.*

They say, *You're weird.* You say, *Yes.*

They say, *You're a geek.* You say, *You betcha.*

WHAT YOU CAN DO

1. You may have found it hard to admit to yourself and others that you are gifted because it seems arrogant and because you know how much you don't know. Now that you have read this book, you might have to admit that you have a rainforest mind. Make a list of the benefits that you can now acknowledge. Draw a mind map of your strengths. Give yourself permission to feel proud of your traits and accomplishments.

2. Who do you know who would celebrate your rainforest-mindedness with you? Share this book with that person, and let yourself be more vulnerable than usual. See how it feels to talk about some of your abilities and achievements with a person who is able to appreciate them.

Epilogue

A Love Letter to You and Your Rainforest Mind

Dearest.

Yes, you. With that dazzlingly intense rainforest mind.

You have so much courage.

To be here, on this planet, during such tumultuous times. To stay sensitive, empathetic, and compassionate. To perceive and feel the layers of human suffering, despair, rage, fear, and sorrow. To stay open to your deepest emotions. To speak out against injustice. To develop your intuitive abilities even when not knowing might make your life easier.

You have so much strength.

To be willing to face your demons. To persistently uncover the painful patterns of shame, depression, and anxiety handed down to you from your parents and their parents before them. To unravel the legacy of abuse within your ancestral line so that the generations after you experience greater self-acceptance and inner peace. To understand

and process your fear and rage. To choose the extraordinarily long, hard road of introspection and analysis so that you might live authentically and compassionately and so that all children might have better lives.

You have so much intellect.

To allow your curiosity to run free through the multiple pathways of your effervescent layers. To gobble up as much learning as you can manage. To know that "you think too much" translates into "you breathe too much" and, no, there can never be too much thinking. To use your capacity to problem solve for healing yourself, your family, and your community while maintaining healthy boundaries and limits and making time for the seventeen books piled next to your bed.

You have so much sensitivity.

To appreciate and trust the intricate beauty and power of the natural world. To maintain your idealism and optimism in spite of the evidence. To let your awarenesses enhance your creativity. To persist in finding your particular art form as a way to express and soothe your sweet soul and the soul of the world.

You have so much spirit.

To keep looking for love in spite of the bullies. In spite of your difficulty communicating with the multitudes of slower, simpler thinkers. In spite of your lonely heart. To expand your awareness into the invisible world. To receive the powerful love and guidance from the universe. To build your particularly rainforest-y spiritual practice. To allow yourself to become all that you can be— more than you ever thought possible.

More than you ever thought possible.

Dear One. Yes, you. With that dazzlingly intense rainforest mind.

You. Are. Loved.

Further Reading and Resources

BOOKS

Allanketner, Anne. *Spells of Mending.*

Aron, Elaine. *The Highly Sensitive Person.*

Baldwin, Christina. *Life's Companion: Journal Writing as Spiritual Quest.*

Blackstone, Judith. *Belonging Here: A Guide for the Spiritually Sensitive Person.*

Boldt, Lawrence. *Zen and the Art of Making a Living.*

Bourne, Edmund. *The Anxiety and Phobia Workbook.*

Burka, Jane and Leora Yuen. *Procrastination.*

Clynes, Tom. *The Boy Who Played With Fusion: Extreme Science, Extreme Parenting and How to Make a Star.*

Daniels, Susan and Michael Piechowski, eds. *Living with Intensity.*

Davis, Joy Lawson. *Bright, Talented, and Black: A Guide for Families of African American Gifted Learners.*

Fiedler, Ellen, *Bright Adults: Uniqueness and Belonging across the Lifespan.*

Hayes, Melanie. *We Tried Normal: 2e Family Stories.*

Jacobsen, Mary-Elaine. *The Gifted Adult.*

Kennedy, Diane and Rebecca Cull. *Bright Not Broken: Gifted Kids, ADHD, and Autism.*

Kennedy-Moore, Eileen. *Smart Parenting for Smart Kids.*

Kerr, Barbara and Sanford Cohn. *Smart Boys: Talent, Manhood, and the Search for Meaning.*

Kerr, Barbara. *Smart Girls in the Twenty-First Century: Understanding Talented Girls and Women.*

Medina, Carmen and Lois Kelly. *Rebels at Work.*

Nauta, Noks. *Gifted Workers: Hitting the Target.*

Noble, Kathleen. *Riding the Windhorse: Spiritual Intelligence and the Growth of the Self.*

Prober, Paula. *Your Rainforest Mind: A Guide to the Well-Being of Gifted Adults and Youth.*

Sher, Barbara. *Refuse to Choose.*

Silverman, Linda. *Giftedness 101.*

Streznewski, Marylou. *Gifted Grownups.*

Tolan, Stephanie, ed. *Off the Charts: Asynchrony and the Gifted Child.*

Wapnick, Emilie. *How to Be Everything.*

Webb, James et al. *Misdiagnosis and Dual Diagnoses of Gifted Children and Adults.*

Young, Valerie. *The Secret Thoughts of Successful Women.*

WEBSITES

drdanpeters.com
(psychologist, articles, videos from Dan Peters)

gailpost.com
(psychologist, blog from Gail Post)

highability.org
(articles and resources from Douglas Eby)

hoagiesgifted.org
(articles, resources, blogs)

intergifted.com
(articles, resources, Facebook group)

nagc.org
(National Association for Gifted Children)

puttylike.com
(support for multipotentiality)

rainforestmind.com
(my blog)

sengifted.org
(Supporting the Emotional Needs of the Gifted)

thegwordfilm.com
(documentary about giftedness due out 2020)

theschooloflife.com
(resources for mental health; online community)

animas.org
(supporting mental health through programs in nature)

gifteddevelopment.com
(Linda Silverman's Center, Denver, CO)

MUSIC

Courage by Pink

Empathy by Alanis Morissette

You Will Be Found from *Dear Evan Hansen*

This Is Me from *The Greatest Showman*

Shine by Tracy Bonham

Index

A

achievement pressure
  and doubting one's own
    giftedness, 16, 27, 30–31
  and gender, 29
  and multipotentiality, 67, 72
  and perfectionism, 74, 79–80, 86
  and procrastination, 84
  and rainforest mind
    identification, 1, 10–11
  and teen experience, 23
ADHD (attention deficit disorder).
  See misdiagnosis
affirmations, 133
Ally McBeal, 95
Animas Institute, 96
Antrim, Donald, 71
anxiety. *See* worry
The Anxiety and Phobia Workbook
  (Bourne), 51, 87
Argentine tango, 93, 96
art. *See* creativity

B

Baldwin, Christina, 97
bipolar disorder. *See* misdiagnosis
Boldt, Laurence, 73
boundaries
  and overwhelm, 55
  and perfectionism, 77, 78, 86
  and sensitivity, 40, 44
  and social responsibility, 112–113
Bourne, Edmund, 51, 87
Bowman, Katy, 51
Boyd, Andrew, 38–39
The Boy Who Played with Fusion
  (Clynes), 130
Brain Pickings, 93–94
bullying, 3–4, 15, 28
Burka, Jane, 84–85

C

Cain, Susan, 61
Calm (app), 44
career choices
  and acceptance of rainforest
    mind, 150
  and doubting one's own
    giftedness, 17
  and multipotentiality, 31, 63–68,
    72
  and rainforest mind needs, 4
CBT (cognitive behavioral therapy),
  87
chain saw families. *See* family of
  origin issues
childhood. *See* family of origin issues;
  school experiences
Clynes, Tom, 130
cognitive behavioral therapy (CBT),
  87
college, 22–23, 28, 79
compassion fatigue, 38–39
connectedness, 38–39, 43
counseling, 135–145
  and doubting one's own
    giftedness, 25, 34–35
  finding a therapist, 142–143
  information for therapists,
    139–142
  and multipotentiality, 73
  and overwhelm, 61–62
  and parenting, 122, 123, 127,
    134, 142
  and perfectionism, 78, 88–89
  and rainforest mind
    identification, 13–14, 140–141
  and relationships, 97–98
  and sensitivity, 45
  and social responsibility, 114,
    135–136
  strategies for, 144–145
  and worry, 52

A Counsel of Resistance and Delight in the Face of Fear (Shaw), 115–116

creativity
  benefits of, 148
  and doubting one's own giftedness, 28
  and relationships, 98
  and sensitivity, 40, 44
  and social responsibility, 117, 118–119
  and worry, 47

criticism, 28. *See also* family of origin issues; others' reactions

Cross, Tracy, 130

Crossing the Unknown Sea: Work as a Pilgrimage of Identity (Whyte), 73

D

Dabrowski, Kazimierz, 45

decision-making
  and doubting one's own giftedness, 16–17
  and multipotentiality, 63, 68–71
  and rainforest mind identification, 10
  strategies for, 70–71

denial. *See* doubting one's own giftedness

depression, 19

depth psychology, 144–145

dialogues, inner
  and decision-making, 70
  and impostor syndrome, 106
  and perfectionism, 88
  and relationships, 98
  and social responsibility, 117–118
  and worry, 51

disappointment/frustration with others, 53, 54
  and multipotentiality, 56
  and perfectionism, 102–104, 106
  and rainforest mind identification, 9, 11, 12
  strategies for, 60–62

Diving into the Wreck (Rich), 139

Dixie Chicks, 103

doubting one's own giftedness, 15–19, 26–35
  and early experiences, 27–29
  and impostor syndrome, 27, 30, 99–101
  and rainforest mind identification, 1, 12, 14
  soliloquy on, 15–19
  strategies, 24–25, 34–35
  and teen experience, 131
  See also impostor syndrome

Dweck, Carol, 87

E

elitism concerns, 5, 8, 28, 30. *See also* social responsibility

emotional intelligence, 37–38

emotions
  and emotional intelligence, 37, 38
  and parenting, 121, 133–134
  strategies for, 42
  and teen experience, 20–21
  See also sensitivity

empathy, 10, 38–39, 148. *See also* sensitivity

empoweryou.com, 73

ethical concerns. *See* elitism concerns; social responsibility

exercise, 42, 51

existential depression, 21, 130–132. *See also* social responsibility

extroversion, 61

F

failure. *See* fear of failure

family of origin issues
  and decision-making, 69
  and doubting one's own giftedness, 28
  and magnificence, 110
  and overwhelm, 54
  and parenting, 120, 122, 123, 134
  and perfectionism, 74, 88
  and resilience, 138
  and sensitivity, 42, 45
  and social responsibility, 112

and worry, 46, 47
See also counseling
fear of failure, 104–105
    and accepting mistakes, 104–105,
    106, 107
    and decision-making, 70
    and perfectionism, 75
    and rainforest mind
    identification, 1, 11
    and teen experience, 21
    See also impostor syndrome
fitting in. *See* relationships
4pt0.org, 128
friendship. *See* relationships
frustration. *See* disappointment/
    frustration with others

G

gender
    and doubting one's own
    giftedness, 29
    and impostor syndrome, 106
    and sensitivity, 20, 41
giftedness label
    and doubting one's own
    giftedness, 15–19, 26–27
    and rainforest mind analogy, 5,
    7, 8
    and rainforest mind
    identification, 12
    strategies, 14
guided imagery. *See* visualization

H

Headspace (app), 44
healthjourneys.com, 51, 97
Heartmath, 51
Hoagies Gifted Discussion Group
    (Facebook group), 60–61
hoagiesgifted.org, 145
homeschooling, 128
How to Be Everything (Wapnick), 72
humor, 40, 52, 148

I

images. *See* visualization

imaginary support network, 94–95,
    97, 118
imagination, 12
impatience. *See* disappointment/
    frustration with others
impostor syndrome, 99–101
    and doubting one's own
    giftedness, 27, 30, 99–101
    and perfectionism, 75, 79, 80
    and rainforest mind
    identification, 11
    strategies for, 106
    and teen experience, 22
    See also doubting one's own
    giftedness
Insight Timer (app), 44
intellectual stimulation, need for
    as overthinking, 13, 53, 57–59
    and parenting, 133
    and procrastination, 84
    and rainforest mind
    identification, 11
    and rainforest mind needs, 4
    and teen experience, 19–20
    and worry, 48, 49
intensity, 18, 91, 147–148. *See also*
    sensitivity
Intergifted.com, 96
Internal Family Systems (IFS) model,
    117
introversion, 61
Introvert, Dear (website), 61
intuition
and decision-making, 70
    and doubting one's own
    giftedness, 18
    and rainforest mind
    identification, 10
    and relationships, 96, 97
    and social responsibility, 111, 113

J

journaling
    and counseling, 144
    and parenting, 123, 127
    and perfectionism, 88

and relationships, 97, 98
and sensitivity, 42
and social responsibility, 117–118
and worry, 51
See also strategies

K

Kelly, Lois, 60
Kennedy-Moore, Eileen, 134
"know-it-all." *See* others' reactions

L

learning, ease of
    and doubting one's own
        giftedness, 27, 28, 29
    and fear of failure, 21, 105
    and perfectionism, 74–75, 80
    and teen experience, 21
learning, love of
    and acceptance of rainforest
        mind, 150
    benefits of, 148
    and decision-making, 70
    and doubting one's own
        giftedness, 16
    and multipotentiality, 65, 68
    and rainforest mind
        identification, 1, 10
    and rainforest mind needs, 4
    and teen experience, 19, 20
Life's Companion: Journal Writing as
    Spiritual Quest (Baldwin), 97
listening, 123, 133–134
Living with Intensity (Daniels and
    Piechowski), 45, 133
loneliness, 96
    and acceptance of rainforest
        mind, 150
    and connectedness, 39
    and doubting one's own
        giftedness, 30–31
    and rainforest mind needs, 4
    and teen experience, 21, 130–131
    See also relationships
love letter, 154–156

M

magnificence, 109–110
medical issues, 51–52
Medina, Carmen, 60
meditation
    and decision-making, 70
    and relationships, 97
    and sensitivity, 42, 45
    and worry, 51
Meetup.com, 96
mindmaps, 72. *See also* journaling
Miranda, Lin-Manuel, 40–41, 106
misdiagnosis
    and acceptance of rainforest
        mind, 150
    and counseling, 141–142, 145
    and doubting one's own
        giftedness, 18
    and multipotentiality, 65
    and overwhelm, 62
    and rainforest mind
        identification, 10
Misdiagnosis and Dual Diagnoses
    of Gifted Children and Adults
    (Webb), 62, 145
mistakes, accepting
    and decision-making, 70–71
    and fear of failure, 104–105, 106,
        107
    and parenting, 123–124
    and perfectionism, 87
multipotentiality, 63–73
    benefits of, 148–149
    and career choices, 31, 63–68, 72
    and decision-making, 63, 68–71
    and disappointment/frustration
        with others, 56
    and doubting one's own
        giftedness, 31
    and rainforest mind needs, 4
    strategies for, 72–73
myths about gifted people
    and doubting one's own
        giftedness, 16, 17
    ease, 3, 4, 146–147

and impostor syndrome, 99
and multipotentiality, 63–64, 68
and school experiences, 34
See also others' reactions

N

NAGC (National Association for
Gifted Children), 128
National Association for Gifted
Children (NAGC), 128
nature, responses to
and decision-making, 70
and rainforest mind
identification, 10
and relationships, 96
and teen experience, 22
Noble, Kathleen D., 116
"not enough," 1, 12
NuMinds, 128

O

OCD (obsessive-compulsive
disorder). *See* misdiagnosis
OEs (overexcitabilities), 41–43, 45,
133
others' reactions
and acceptance of rainforest
mind, 149, 151–152
and disappointment, 104
and doubting one's own
giftedness, 16, 24, 28, 29, 30, 146
and elitism concerns, 8
overthinking, 16, 53, 58
and overwhelm, 54, 56
and perfectionism, 82, 103–104
and rainforest mind analogy, 18
and rainforest mind
identification, 1, 11
and school experiences, 15, 28,
101–102, 126
and sensitivity, 36, 37
and teen experience, 131
"too much," 1, 5
and work environment, 17
See also myths about gifted people

overexcitabilities (OEs), 41–43, 45,
133
overthinking, 16, 53, 57–59
overwhelm, 53–62
and acceptance of rainforest
mind, 150–151
and boundaries, 54–55
contradictions of, 53, 55–57
and decision-making, 69
and doubting one's own
giftedness, 30–31
and overexcitabilities, 42
and overthinking, 53, 57–59
and rainforest mind
identification, 9, 12, 13
and rainforest mind needs, 4
strategies for, 60–62
and waiting, 129–130
See also sensitivity

P

parenting, 120–134
and adolescence, 122, 124–125
and counseling, 122, 123, 127,
134, 142
and decision-making, 70
and doubting one's own
giftedness, 17
and existential depression,
130–132
and multipotentiality, 72
and perfectionism, 87–88
and school experiences, 125–128
strategies for, 60–61, 126–128,
133–134
and worry, 52
Parenting Gifted Children (Facebook
group), 60–61
perfectionism, 74–89
and acceptance of rainforest
mind, 150
and being driven, 77–78
benefits of, 148
and disappointment in others,
102–104, 106

and doubting one's own
giftedness, 17–18, 27, 28
healthy, 74, 78, 81–83
and others' reactions, 82, 103–104
and procrastination, 79, 80, 83–85
and rainforest mind
identification, 10
roots of, 74–76
strategies for, 86–89
and teen experience, 22
Perfectionism (Burka and Yuen),
84–85
Pips (imaginary support network),
94–95, 97, 118
Plotkin, Bill, 108–109
Popova, Maria, 93–94
praise
and doubting one's own
giftedness, 27
and fear of failure, 105
and perfectionism, 74, 75, 80, 87
procrastination
and doubting one's own
giftedness, 27
and perfectionism, 79, 80, 83–85
and rainforest mind
identification, 1, 11
psychotherapy. *See* counseling
PTSD (post-traumatic stress
syndrome), 52
puttylike.com, 73

Q

Quiet, 61

R

racism, 28
rainforest minds
acceptance of, 31, 66, 92, 101,
149–152
analogy, 4–5, 8–9, 13–14, 18
benefits of, 146–149, 153
description of, 1–2
identification of, 1, 9–12, 13–14,
125, 140–141
love letter to, 154–156

misunderstanding of, 2–3
needs of, 3–4, 32–33
resources for, 157–160
Rebels at Work (Medina and Kelly), 60
Refuse to Choose (Sher), 66
relationships, 90–98
and acceptance of rainforest
mind, 92, 150, 153
and boundaries, 113
and doubting one's own
giftedness, 15, 31
and imaginary support network,
94–95, 97
and overwhelm, 56, 57
and parenting, 127
and perfectionism, 82
and rainforest mind
identification, 11
strategies for, 42, 96–98
and teen experience, 21, 130–131
See also disappointment/
frustration with others; loneliness
research, love of. *See* learning, love of
resources, 157–160
Reznick, Charlotte, 126
Rich, Adrienne, 139
Riding the Windhorse (Noble), 116

S

saving the world. *See* social
responsibility
saying no. *See* boundaries
school experiences
and doubting one's own
giftedness, 15–16, 27, 28, 34
and others' reactions, 15, 28,
101–102, 126
and parenting, 125–128
and perfectionism, 75, 79
and procrastination, 84
and rainforest mind
identification, 1
and rainforest mind needs, 3–4
strategies for, 126–128
and teen experience, 19–20
and waiting, 15, 128–130

The School of Life, 96, 145
The Secret Thoughts of Successful Women (Young), 106
self-soothing techniques, 42, 44
SENG (Supporting the Emotional Needs of the Gifted), 128
sengifted.org, 145
sensitivity, 36–43
　and acceptance of rainforest mind, 150
　benefits of, 147
　and doubting one's own giftedness, 28
　and emotional intelligence, 37–38
　misunderstanding of, 36
　and overexcitabilities, 41–43
　and parenting, 121–122
　and rainforest mind identification, 9
　and rainforest mind needs, 4
　and relationships, 91
　and social responsibility, 38–39, 42–43
　strategies for, 40–41, 44–45
　and teen experience, 20–21
　and worry, 46, 49
　See also emotions
service, desire for. *See* social responsibility
sexism, 28
Shaw, Martin, 115–116
Sher, Barbara, 66
siblings, 28
Smart Parenting for Smart Kids (Kennedy-Moore), 134
social responsibility, 108–119
　and acceptance of rainforest mind, 150
　benefits of, 149
　and boundaries, 112–113
　and connectedness, 38–39
　and counseling, 114, 135–136
　and decision-making, 69
　and doubting one's own giftedness, 17, 29

　and impostor syndrome, 100
　and magnificence, 109–110
　and rainforest mind identification, 11
　and sensitivity, 38–39, 42–43
　strategies for, 117–119
　and teen experience, 21–22, 131
　and worry, 47
spirituality
　and decision-making, 70
　and rainforest mind identification, 10
　and relationships, 95
　and sensitivity, 45
　and social responsibility, 114–116
　and worry, 49
standards. *See* perfectionism
Star Wars, 116
strategies
　counseling, 144–145
　decision-making, 70–71
　disappointment/frustration with others, 60–62
　doubting one's own giftedness, 24–25, 34–35
　fear of failure, 105, 107
　impostor syndrome, 106
　multipotentiality, 72–73
　overwhelm, 60–62
　parenting, 60–61, 126–128, 133–134
　perfectionism, 86–89
　rainforest mind identification, 13–14, 24
　relationships, 42, 96–98
　school experiences, 126–128
　sensitivity, 40–41, 44–45
　worry, 51–52
Supporting the Emotional Needs of the Gifted (SENG), 128

T

teen experience, 19–23, 122, 124–125, 130–132
therapy. *See* counseling

Tippett, Krista, 94
"too much," 1, 5, 12, 41. *See also*
    intensity; overwhelm
twice exceptionality (2e), 142, 145

V

visualization
    and parenting, 126
    and relationships, 97
    and sensitivity, 42, 45
    and worry, 51

W

waiting, 12, 15, 128–130
Wapnick, Emilie, 64, 66, 72
Webb, James, 63, 145
Whitman, Walt, 55
Whyte, David, 68, 73
Wise Self, 118–119
wonder, 49
work environment
    and doubting one's own
    giftedness, 17
    and perfectionism, 77–78
    and sensitivity, 42
    strategies for, 60
    and waiting, 129
worry, 46–52
    and doubting one's own
    giftedness, 16
    strategies for, 51–52
    and teen experience, 21, 131

Y

Young, Valerie, 106
*Your Rainforest Mind: A Guide to the
    Well-Being of Gifted Adults and
    Youth* (Prober), 6, 134
Yuen, Lenora, 84–85

Z

Zen and the Art of Making a Living
    (Boldt), 73

Made in United States
Troutdale, OR
05/13/2024

19851272R00100